SEA TURTLES

© Kendra Choquette-D'Avella

AN ECOLOGICAL GUIDE

DAVE GULKO & KAREN ECKERT

Recommended for use by the Curriculum Research & Development Group (CRDG) of the University of Hawaiʻi as a companion text to their Fluid Earth/Living Ocean Marine Science Program, and with other science courses dealing with marine science in middle schools, high schools, universities and colleges.

MUTUAL PUBLISHING

"A turtle is more than just what is inside its shell – it is only really a turtle when accompanied by its environment"

– Roderic Mast, Conservation International

© Ursula Keuper-Bennett/Peter Bennett

© Dave Gulko

ACKNOWLEDGEMENTS

A book of this scope is only possible because scientists and enthusiasts throughout the world have labored for many decades to bring the complex ecology of sea turtles to light. In addition to relying heavily on the published works of these experts, we are deeply grateful to Scott Eckert, Mark Heckman, Carol Hopper, and Mary Pickett, for their comprehensive reviews of earlier drafts. We would also like to thank George Balazs, Karen Bjorndal, Sneed Collard, Michael Coyne, Ken Dodd, Marydele Donnelly, Peter Dutton, Emery Eckert, Jeffrey Graham, Skippy Hau, Steve Kolinski, Dave Levenson, Ken Lohmann, Peter Lutz, Anne Meylan, John Mitchell, Sara Peck, R. P. Ross, Barbara Schroeder, Jeff Seminoff, Kartik Shanker, Donna Shaver-Miller, Thierry Work, and George Zug for their valued input into specific sections. In a lot of ways the photos in this book tell the majority of the story, often in a form that could never be accomplished with words or simple graphics. We're indebted to Zoè M. Bass, Kendra Choquette-D'Avella, Didiher Chacón, Steve Cornelius, Scott Eckert, Jeffrey Graham, Skippy Hau, Chris Johnson, Ursula Keuper-Bennett, Jeff Kuwabara, Wendy Murray, Kim Peyton, Robert L. Pitman, Peter C. H. Pritchard, David Schrichte, Jennifer Smith, Robert Thorne, and Thierry Work for providing the phenomenal photos you will see throughout this book. Unless stated otherwise, all graphics were designed by Dave Gulko. Finally, but most importantly, we'd like to thank Shahin Ansari and Scott Eckert for the encouragement and emotional re-charging they supplied during the production of this work.

Sea Turtles: An Ecological Guide

Table of Contents

GETTING THE MOST FROM THIS BOOK

This book is designed such that it may be just as easily used by those who are a novice to the ways of ecology and sea turtles as those who are experts. Regardless of background, we hope that readers will get something different out of it each time they go through it. We have tried to design it to be visually interesting yet factual, so that it can be used as a ready resource. Most importantly, it is hoped that by showing how complex and intricate many of the interactions and behaviors are that occur among and between sea turtles and their neighbors, our readers will work harder to protect not just the animal but the ecosystems that sustain us all, at the level of influencing their friends, their community, and their local, state and federal governments.

A Word About Scientific "Lingo":

Every effort has been made to represent information in everyday language and still retain the accuracy of the information. Where scientific language is heavily used, drawings are often incorporated to assist in understanding the material. Additionally, there is a full Glossary (Appendix III) at the back of the book. If you come upon a word in **bold** that you're not sure about, look it up quickly in the Glossary. We hope that through your readings and musings with this book you'll learn a new word or two and, perhaps more importantly, focus instead on the processes and relationships described.

Theory vs Fact:

OK, let's face it, if all we did was present to you that which we know to be absolute fact this would be a much shorter book. One of the most interesting things about studying ecology, and certainly this is true about sea turtles, is that there is still so much that we do not fully understand. Some of the current theories presented in this book may not have been extensively tested. Still, it is felt that by introducing you to some of the theories and research currently ongoing in the study of sea turtles, you will gain a greater appreciation of the complex ecology of these ancient animals. To minimize confusion, the following symbol ⓣ is used throughout the book to denote material that comes from untested scientific theories.

Layout of the Book:

By the time most people get around to reading the Introduction section of a book, they've already flipped through the book a couple times (it's OK to admit it). The first thing you'll notice is that this book is very visual, full of graphics and drawings. Often there is only minimum text associated with these diagrams; believe it or not, this was done on purpose. In essence, you become drawn into trying to work your way through the diagrams and by way of this process you get to go through the wonder of 'Discovery' ("Oh wow, now I get it!"), which is probably one of the most magical things about science, no matter what your background.

Additional Features:

Endangered Status:

Sea turtle species are classified both internationally (following the World Conservation Union (IUCN) rating system) and nationally, such as by the U.S. Endangered Species Act. Look for the small globe of the world 🌐 for the IUCN rating (Data Deficient, Vulnerable, Endangered, or Critically Endangered), and the small U.S. flag 🏴 for the U.S. rating (Threatened, Endangered).

Turtle Icons:

Most pages bring together and synthesize a lot of material in order to provide an overview of the concept discussed. But sometimes we focus very specifically on a particular type of sea turtle, and when that happens we will let you know by the presence of a small sea turtle graphic found in the corner of certain pages. These graphics serve to identify the species of sea turtle(s) to which the information on that page primarily refers. If no turtle graphic is present, the information applies generally to most or all sea turtles. The following letters inside the graphic will be used to represent the most common hard-shelled species:

G = Green Sea Turtle
H = Hawksbill Sea Turtle

L = Loggerhead Sea Turtle
K = Kemp's Ridley Sea Turtle
O = Olive Ridley Sea Turtle

Leatherback Sea Turtle

Look for this leatherback graphic when the information pertains to this unusual species.

The Big Picture Pages:

Brings together and synthesizes a lot of material in order to show a larger representation of what's going on.

Subject Bibliography:

Appendix IV is an annotated bibliography of related books followed by a subject bibliography of scientific papers where you can find additional sources of information on specific topics of interest.

The Infographic: The Infographic is a concentrated informational graphic designed to give the reader visual data on the ecology of the organism being featured. As shown in the example below, each section is labeled and provides specific information. Please refer to the guide below as a key to the different sections.

(1) Adult Diet: Major food types are shown and identified below; where applicable, the dominant food item is labeled. More detailed information on feeding ecology can be found on pages 37 - 44.

(2) Global Distribution Map: Shows global distribution of the highlighted species. The capital letter "N" (for nesting) is used to indicate major nesting rookeries on the distribution map, whereas the shading indicates the approximate global range of all life history stages for each species.

(3) Primary Threats: Shows primary human-associated threats to the survival of featured species. For more information on human impacts, see pages 84 - 101.

(4) Carapace Characteristics: Each sea turtle species has a unique arrangement of **scutes** that make up the carapace (shell). The upper right corner of each sea turtle infographic contains a diagram of that species' characteristic carapace.

(5) Life History Table: Broken into five sections representing the following life history stages: Mating, Nesting, Incubation (of eggs in nest), Juvenile, and Adult. Information at the bottom of the Nesting section documents the range of average clutch sizes around the world; black background shading indicates mostly night-time turtle nesting, no black background indicates mostly daytime nesting. Numbers at the bottom of the Incubation section refer to the average egg development period in days. Because sea turtles typically spend their first 2-7 years in the open sea, and it's only later that some species return to coastal zones, the Juvenile box highlights any differences in habitat utilization between early and late juvenile stages. The number at the bottom of the Adult section is the typical number of years to reach sexual maturity, if known.

(6) Predators: Common predators on the organism featured and identified below. The panel is divided into three sections, which from left to right represent: the Egg & Hatchling Stages, the Juvenile Stage, and the Adult Stage. More information on sea turtle predators can be found on pages 45 - 50. Note that these represent common predators but by no means every predator.

Predators & Prey:

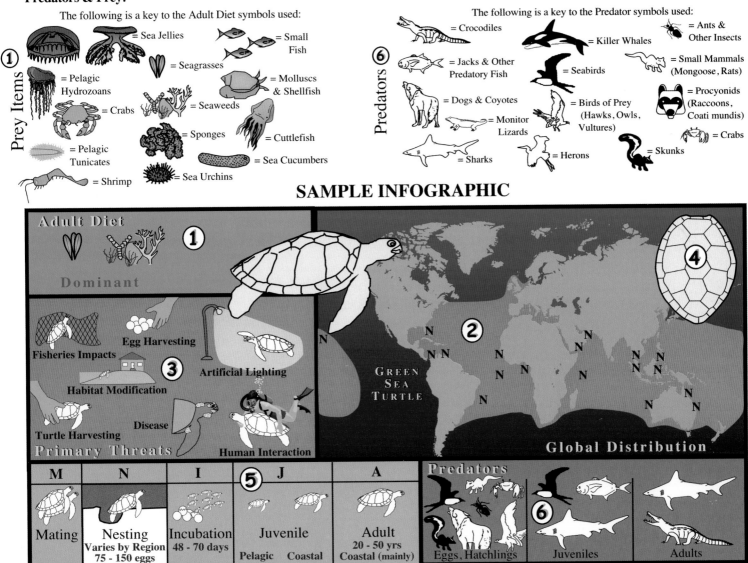

The following is a key to the Adult Diet symbols used:

Prey Items
= Sea Jellies
= Small Fish
= Seagrasses
= Pelagic Hydrozoans
= Molluscs & Shellfish
= Crabs
= Seaweeds
= Sponges
= Cuttlefish
= Pelagic Tunicates
= Sea Cucumbers
= Sea Urchins
= Shrimp

The following is a key to the Predator symbols used:

Predators
= Crocodiles
= Killer Whales
= Ants & Other Insects
= Jacks & Other Predatory Fish
= Seabirds
= Small Mammals (Mongoose, Rats)
= Dogs & Coyotes
= Birds of Prey (Hawks, Owls, Vultures)
= Procyonids (Raccoons, Coati mundis)
= Monitor Lizards
= Crabs
= Sharks
= Herons
= Skunks

SAMPLE INFOGRAPHIC

Adult Diet
(1)
Dominant
Fisheries Impacts
Egg Harvesting
(3)
Artificial Lighting
Habitat Modification
Disease
Turtle Harvesting
Human Interaction
Primary Threats

(2) GREEN SEA TURTLE
Global Distribution
(4)

M	N	I	(5) J	A
Mating	Nesting Varies by Region 75 - 150 eggs	Incubation 48 - 70 days	Juvenile Pelagic Coastal	Adult 20 - 50 yrs Coastal (mainly)

Predators
(6)
Eggs, Hatchlings | Juveniles | Adults

While often characterized as solitary animals, at various stages of their life history, sea turtles are rather social (see pages 58, 59, 67, 72).

INTRODUCTION

This book looks at the world of sea turtles in terms of their roles in the ecosystem. It explores their natural history (pages 17-24, 37-75), their life and times (pages 25-36), and their struggles against the threats posed by man (pages 79-101). It looks at their role as predators (pages 37-44) and prey (pages 45-50, 81-83), as competitors (page 78, 89) and hosts (pages 51-55), and as conduits for energy and nutrient movement through the environment (pages 44, 69) in which they live; in essence their ecology.

What Is This Thing Called Ecology?

Ecology is the study of interactions between an organism and its environment (both physical and biological).

All living organisms interact in some way with their environment.

Interactions may involve members of their own species...

...as well as other species.

Within their biological environments, organisms can be organized into distinct groupings:

Species
A natural group of organisms that can interbreed.

Population
All of the individuals of a species within a defined area.

Community
Several different populations occurring together within a defined area.

?

All of these can live and interact within an **ecosystem**: A biological community (or series of communities) plus all of the non-living components of an environment. Often ecosystems are characterized by biological interactions such as predation, competition, symbiotic relationships, and physical interactions involving energy sources, climate, and nutrient and mineral cycling. The ecological role of a single species within a community is called a **niche**.

Levels of Organization

Ecosystem = All communities of living organisms plus the non-living (physical, chemical, etc.) components with which they interact within an environment.

Biosphere = all of the earth's ecosystems.

Community = Populations of different types of animals and plants within a defined area.

Population = All the animals or plants of a specific type within a defined area.

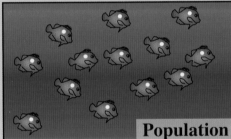

Each of these levels contains interactions between organisms and their environment, and each level can be looked at as the sum of the processes (both biological and physical) that occur within it and those that occur between it and surounding systems. Thus **ecology** can be looked at in a variety of different ways, depending upon one's perspective. In this book we will strive to look at the ecology of sea turtles at the organism, community, and ecosystem levels.

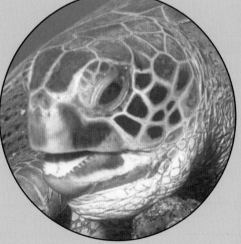

Organism = An individual animal or plant.

A Maidu Folktale

In the beginning there was no light, and everywhere there was water.

From the north a raft came, carrying Turtle. A feather rope fell down from the sky. Earth Starter came down the rope, tied it to the raft, and boarded it. He wore a mask, but through it his face shone like the very sun. Earth Starter sat there quietly, looking at Turtle.

"Where did you come from?" Turtle asked.

"From way up there," said Earth Starter, pointing at the sky.

"I would like it if you would make me some dry land to stand on now and then," said Turtle. "Will you be putting people on the earth?"

"Yes, I will," Earth Starter replied.

"When will you do that?"

"Sometime. If you want me to make you some dry land, though, you will have to get me some earth."

Turtle got ready to dive under the water to find some earth. Earth Starter tied a rock around Turtle's wrist and tied the feather rope to Turtle's leg.

"If the rope is not long enough, I'll give it a single tug," Turtle said. "If it is long enough, I'll get some earth and then tug on the rope twice, and then you can pull me up."

Then he dove over the side. But he stayed down there under the water for six years. When he came up he was covered with mud. He had only a little bit of earth, stuck under his claws. Earth Starter scraped this earth from Turtleís claws and rolled it in his hands. The little ball grew and grew until it was as big as the world.

"Good," said Turtle. "Now can you make some light?"

So Earth Starter called his sister, the Sun, from the east, and his brother, the Moon, from the west. And so the earth and its light were created.

Anthropologist A. E. Kroeber recorded this creation myth of the Maidu, a native people of central California, in the early 1900s. Source: McNamee, G and Urrea, LA (1996). Johnson Books, Boulder, CO. Used with permission.

Reptile Characteristics

Sea turtles belong to the Class Reptilia (derived from the Latin word meaning "to creep"), which also includes crocodilians, snakes, lizards and their ancient relatives, the dinosaurs; some experts also include birds in this group (but that's a whole other story). Millions and millions of years ago, reptiles were among the first large animals to be able to live on land, away from sources of water, for extended periods of time. Many of the characteristics seen in ocean-voyaging sea turtles are a result of the early reptiles adapting to a dry, terrestrial (land) existence.

All reptiles share the following characteristics:

• Vertebral Column (spinal column) – mammals, birds, fish, reptiles and amphibians are called "vertebrates" because they have a vertebral column and other shared traits. The spinal column assists in supporting the body, which is especially important in a terrestrial environment.

• Epidermal Scales – scales serve to protect the underlying muscles and other internal organs and reduce water loss.

• Air Breathing – reptiles respire through their lungs. Reptiles are not fish; they do not have gills.

• Ectothermic (what is often called "Cold-blooded") – meaning that the external environment is the primary source of heat for the body, and this heat is exploited largely through behavioral means (such as by basking).

• Internal Fertilization – the fertilization of eggs by sperm occurs inside the female.

Many reptiles (and all sea turtles) lay eggs. In fact, the evolution of the shelled egg (what scientists call the "amniotic egg") paved the way for reptiles to become the first truly land animals. Fish and many amphibians must be in water in order to successfully reproduce. The magical, mystical shelled egg changed all that ("It's not just for breakfast any more…").

Marine Reptiles

There are about 7300 species of reptiles found throughout the world in three major taxonomic "orders":
- Order Crocodylia (alligators and crocodiles ~ 23 species)
- Order Testudines (turtles ~ 285 species)
- Order Squamata (lizards and snakes ~ 7200 species)

As vertebrate animals, all reptiles have a backbone. Reptiles are primarily **ectothermic**, meaning that they maintain their body temperature within fairly narrow limits by behavioral means, as opposed to generating heat internally (like you and I do). Reptiles breathe air. They have either scales or modified scales externally. Many species have claws. They have internal fertilization. Many reptiles have a single bone in their middle ear that conducts sound vibrations to the inner ear. Most reptiles are **oviparous**, laying eggs externally (outside their body) in which their offspring develop.

© Kendra Choquette-D'Avella

Each of the major reptile orders has marine representatives. As with the sea turtles, the other marine reptiles are thought to represent animals whose ancestors left the land and re-adapted to life in the ocean.

© David Schriche

© Jeffrey Graham

© Scott A. Eckert

© Ursula Keuper-Bennett/Peter Bennett

© Jeffrey Graham

© David Schriche

© Robert Thorn

Marine Iguana *(Amblyrhynchus cristatus)*

The only sea-going lizards are the marine iguana (*Amblyrhynchus cristatus*) of the Galapagos Islands; though as marine reptiles go, this group has the weakest association with the ocean. All of their social interactions occur on land. Efficient swimmers, marine iguana propel themselves through the water by undulating their long flattened tails, much like crocodiles. Large adult males can reach lengths of 5 feet (1.5 m). The animals themselves have a grey or black coloration and a more blunt snout than land iguanas.

Diet: Primarily herbivores, marine iguanas often graze on marine algal turf associated with intertidal and nearshore environments. Their diet is supplemented by crustaceans, grasshoppers and the occasional sea lion afterbirth or carrion. Most of these animals focus their underwater feeding on species of red and green algae, such as *Ulva*, *Spermothamnium*, *Centroceras*, and *Gelidium*. Male marine iguanas have been documented diving as deep as 12 m (40 feet) to graze. Populations of these animals on different islands in the Galapagos chain show differences in body size; this is thought to be connected to food abundance, which varies with differences in sea water temperature associated with island locations. As an adaptation to a high salt diet, marine lizards have salt glands located above their eyes and connected to openings in

© Kendra Choquette-D'Avella

their nostrils through a series of ducts. Elimination of excess salt is as simple as sneezing (literally), though this has the side effect of giving their heads a rather salt-encrusted appearance.

Behavior: Early in the day, iguanas openly **bask** on the rocks, soaking up the sun's warmth; it is this stored-up heat energy that allows the iguana to actively forage in cold near-shore waters. Their dark coloration assists in absorbing solar energy during basking. Marine iguanas also show a grouping behavior that is thought to function during the afternoon for thermoregulation and at night to limit mobile parasites from gaining hold.

Males actively defend resting and transit territories and court females from October through January when mating occurs. It is during this time that males adopt a brilliant red and turquoise color in an effort to woo females. Nesting occurs between January and April, usually on softer substrate where the eggs can be buried.

Symbionts: Ornithodoros ticks. Fish have been observed cleaning marine iguanas.

Threats: Hawks, owls, snakes, and crabs prey on eggs and hatchlings. Marine iguanas have evolved anti-predator behavior towards such natural predators, but have not been able to adapt to the presence of feral animals. Given their low reproductive rate, feral cats, dogs and rats pose a major threat to nests and juveniles. Other conservation issues include invasive algae displacing the native seaweeds preferred by iguanas. During the early 1980's the alien algae *Giffordia mitchelliae* started to dominate the intertidal zone and resulted in a noticeable starvation rate in the marine iguana. Pollution is also a threat. Given this species' complete reliance on coastal and intertidal habitat for survival, strong concerns exist about the impacts of even small scale oil spills where these animals occur.

VULNERABLE

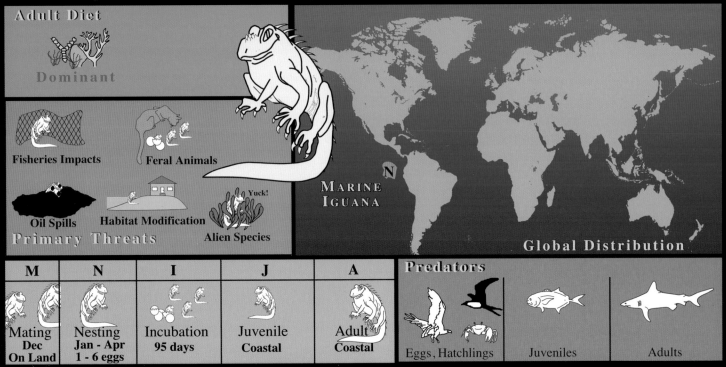

Adult Diet

Dominant

Fisheries Impacts   Feral Animals

Oil Spills   Habitat Modification   Yuck!
Primary Threats   Alien Species

N

MARINE
IGUANA

Global Distribution

M	N	I	J	A
Mating	Nesting	Incubation	Juvenile	Adult
Dec	Jan - Apr	95 days	Coastal	Coastal
On Land	1 - 6 eggs			

Predators

Eggs, Hatchlings	Juveniles	Adults

Saltwater Crocodiles
(*Crocodylus porosus*)

Description:
The difference between alligators and crocodiles is often perplexing for those not facing the jaws of one or the other. Crocodiles have much longer and narrower snouts than do their cousins the alligators. For those that enjoy close-up comparisons, the crocodile's fourth tooth on its lower jaw protrudes visibly upward when its mouth is closed, giving it a kind of sophisticated look prior to snacking time. Both crocodiles and alligators are survivors of the original Archosauria, a frat club which a couple hundred million years ago included the dinosaurs and dominated life all over the planet. Crocodiles and alligators are the most advanced of all living reptiles, many of their features bearing a greater similarity to birds or mammals than they do to other reptiles, such as sea turtles, snakes or lizards.

The saltwater crocodile is the largest of the living reptiles, growing to a length of 33 feet (10 m). Males tend to be larger than females.

Saltwater crocodiles are primarily found around coastal areas (such as mangroves and estuaries) of the southeast Indian Ocean and Pacific regions, but have also been observed swimming in the open ocean between islands in the Pacific.

While possessing salt glands (actually, modified salivary glands) on their tongues, young crocodiles may also drink freshwater when they're at sea. Sometimes this might be done by drinking the thin surface layer of freshwater atop calm seawater after a rain, and reportedly very young crocs may actually snap at rain directly as it falls. Keep in mind the vast majority of the time these animals are drinking saltwater, and active salt glands in adults maintain a proper internal salt balance (see page 23).

© Robert Thorn

🌐 NOT CLASSIFIED

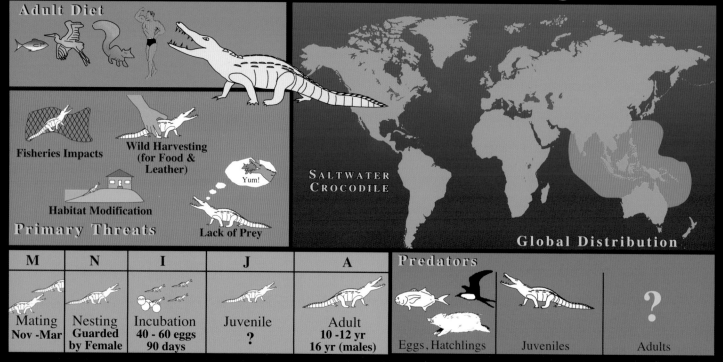

Adult Diet

Primary Threats

Fisheries Impacts

Wild Harvesting (for Food & Leather)

Yum!

Habitat Modification

Lack of Prey

SALTWATER CROCODILE

Global Distribution

M	N	I	J	A
Mating Nov -Mar	Nesting Guarded by Female	Incubation 40 - 60 eggs 90 days	Juvenile ?	Adult 10 -12 yr 16 yr (males)

Predators

Eggs, Hatchlings	Juveniles	Adults ?

Crocs can have up to 32 teeth in the upper jaw, and another 40 in the lower. Their teeth are not well designed for chewing; instead they tend to use them for puncturing, crushing and gripping prey. Occasionally with really large meals, they may first drown the animal (or wayward tourist), and then stuff the carcass somewhere where it can rot for a period of time until it's soft enough to go down easily; though in general they do seem to prefer their food fresh. Though teeth often break off (yours might also if you had a bite force of 3000 lbs/sq. in.!), the crocodile can replace these lost teeth. Interestingly, since crocs lack lips, their mouths tend to leak even when closed.

Diet: Fish, crabs, waterbirds, and small coastal mammals. Some crocodile species are thought to swallow stones for their muscular **gizzard**, where the rocks may assist in breaking-down food and perhaps in altering their bouyancy (ok, that last part has nothing to do with diet, but it is kind of interesting...). Their stomachs are considered to be the most acidic of any vertebrate; as a result, digestion of items that would give you or I heartburn, such as bones and shells, are no problem for the crocodile.

Crocodiles are primarily ambush predators, lying quietly in wait for their prey to come within range. They can use their powerful tails to leap vertically out of the water to grab birds out of the air or pull a mammal off a riverbank or coastline.

Considered by many to be the most fearsome of marine animals, saltwater crocodiles are one of the few creatures that will actually hunt a human. Reportedly, saltwater crocodiles might kill up to 1,000 people per year; most attacks on humans are by large adult males.

Behavior: Male crocodiles may show territorial behavior. Dominant males will occasionally kill subadults that are not large enough to defend a territory themselves or do not leave the freshwater breeding habitats. Mating tends to occur around estuaries and tidal rivers; males are often polygynous, mating with more than one female during a breeding season. Parental care includes nest-guarding behavior by the female and assisting the hatchlings in **pipping** (the process where hatchlings break free of the egg). Crocodiles communicate with each other and their young through vocalization, possessing a larynx (voice box) within their throats like most mammals. Like their cousins the sea turtles, crocodiles do not have X or Y chromosomes; the sex of the offspring is largely determined by the temperature of the nesting environment.

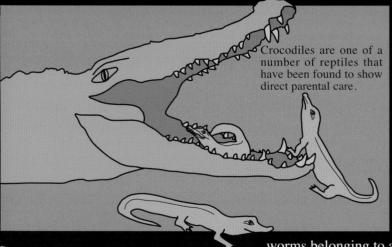

Crocodiles are one of a number of reptiles that have been found to show direct parental care.

Symbionts: internal filarial worms. Rare and unique worms belonging to a group called *Pentastomiasis* occur almost exclusively in the lungs of reptiles, with some species exclusively restricted to the lungs of saltwater crocodiles.

Threats: Crocodiles are hunted for their skin and meat. The saltwater crocodile has an extremely high commercial value compared to other crocodiles due to the lack of ventral osteoderms (bony-like plates), the presence of which makes the tanning process more expensive and difficult. Crocodiles are now commercially farmed in Australia, Papua New Guinea, and Indonesia; however, concerns still exist over wild harvest in many areas.

Sea Snakes

Sea snakes are the most abundant marine reptiles on earth, with approximately 55 species worldwide; there are two subfamilies: the true sea snakes and the sea kraits. Most species are found in coastal waters in Southeast Asia and Northern Australia. One species, the yellow-bellied sea snake (*Pelamis platurus*) is truly pelagic, and occurs in waters throughout the tropical and sub-tropical Indian and Pacific Oceans, including Hawai'i.

Description: Sea snakes are elongate like eels, but can be distinguished by the presence of scales and a flattened, paddle-shaped tail. All true sea snakes give live birth, while the sea kraits crawl ashore to lay eggs. Except for the pelagic Yellow-bellied sea snake, all marine snakes spend a large portion of their time feeding, breeding and resting on or near the bottom. Like sea turtles, they have salt glands for getting rid of excess salt from drinking seawater; though in the case of the sea snake, the gland is located under the tongue.

Sea snakes are capable of staying underwater up to three hours at a time by reducing their metabolic rate. They have a single lung which extends more than two-thirds of their body length. Additional oxygen is directly absorbed through their skin; this extra oxygen displaces some of the nitrogen in their blood, preventing "the bends" on deep dives.

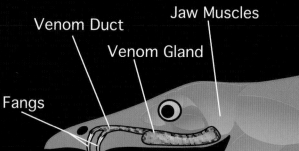

Jaw Muscles

Venom Duct

Venom Gland

Fangs

Venom Components
Hyaluronidase - breaks down tissue, allowing a faster venom effect.

Phospholipase A - effects muscles, impeding prey mobility.

Acetylcholinase - interrupts neuro muscular transmission, slows movement, and interferes with cardiac function and respiration. eventually leading to death.

☠ **Venomous**

🪙 **NOT CLASSIFIED**

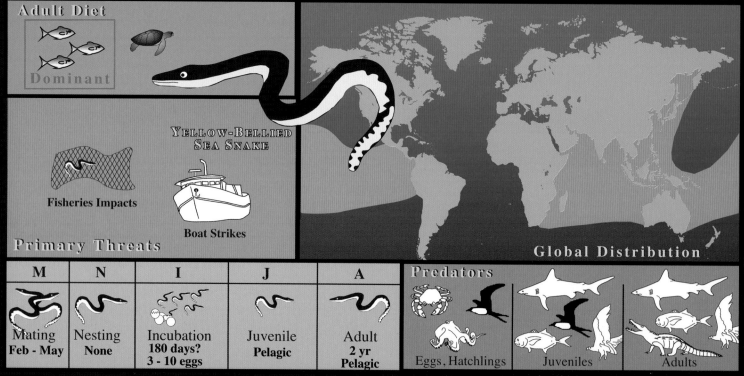

Adult Diet

Dominant

Primary Threats

Fisheries Impacts

Boat Strikes

YELLOW-BELLIED SEA SNAKE

Global Distribution

Predators

M	N	I	J	A
Mating	Nesting	Incubation	Juvenile	Adult
Feb - May	None	180 days? 3 - 10 eggs	Pelagic	2 yr Pelagic

Eggs, Hatchlings

Juveniles

Adults

One of the smaller of the marine snakes, the Yellow-bellied sea snake is completely pelagic and is often found in oceanic **drift lines,** where fish tend to gather near the surface for shelter and end up providing a meal for this marine reptile. As a predator, its primary means of gaining prey is through ambush; it will often quietly lie on the surface and wait for fish to be attracted to it as possible shelter. Its distinctive black and yellow markings have traditionally been viewed as a form of warning coloration; but given its predatory behavior, the markings might also serve to break-up its body form and make it appear more like floating flotsam in the drift line.

Diet: Most sea snakes feed on relatively sedentary fish species, including those that live on the bottom or in reef crevices (e.g. eels and gobies). Three sea snake species specialize in preying on fish eggs. Vibration and taste are their primary senses for hunting. The Yellow-bellied sea snake can snack through a specialized behavior that involves the snake floating at the surface and, in effect, mimicing drift flotsam and thereby attracting small fish seeking shelter. As the snake begins slowly swimming backwards, the fish sheltering beneath it will swim back towards it to regain their lost shelter; in doing so, they are led directly towards the snake's mouth (surprise!). This snake is thought to also prey on hatchling sea turtles that have made their way into pelagic waters.

The venom of certain sea snakes is more deadly than that of rattlesnakes, coral snakes, or the feared cobra. The venom of the Yellow-bellied sea snake is five times more lethal than the cobra's and is a neurotoxin which acts on the prey's musculature. Venom is injected through hollow fangs located on the upper jaw.

The olive sea snake (*Aipysurus laevis*) on the Great Barrier Reef has been shown to possess photosensitivity in its tail; such a reaction may assist the animal in determining if any portion of its tail is exposed when seeking shelter from predators.

Reproduction: Yellow-bellied sea snakes mate annually and give live birth at sea. Males become sexually mature at 50 cm, females at a slightly larger size. Scientists believe that it may require up to two years to reach sexual maturity.

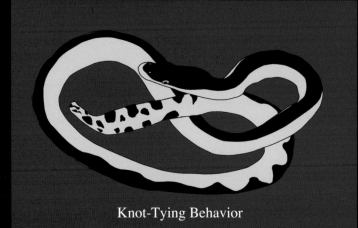

Knot-Tying Behavior

True sea snakes are **ovoviviparous**, giving live birth to snakes that developed inside the female. Unlike mammals, which also give live birth, the sea snake's embryos develop within fertilized, shelled eggs held within the female's body until they hatch. Broods often contain between two and seven young, each up to 20 cm in length.

Neonates and yearlings, as well as subadults and adults (> 35 cm), may congregate under pieces of flotsam, possibly as shelter from both fish and avian predators. Such congregations may facilitate mating. Estimates of first year mortality range from 40 to 90%.

Symbionts: trematodes, bryozoans, barnacles, foraminiferans, hydrozoans, serpulid polychaetes, and bivalves. Most of the externally-attached symbionts are thought to be dislodged when the snake sheds its skin or through the knotting behavior characteristic of these animals.

Predators: Juveniles are preyed upon by birds, pufferfish, octopus & mangrove crabs; subadults & adults are preyed on by birds of prey (sea-eagles, frigate birds), sharks, marine crocodiles, fish (billfish, pufferfish, moray eels, grouper), and marine mammals (leopard seals, bottle-nosed dolphins). Sharks have been extensively studied (in Australia) and shown to be a major predator. The pelagic Yellow-bellied sea snake (*Pelamis platurus*) has few identified predators; even avowed sea snake consumers such as a variety of pufferfish species will not willingly attack *P. platurus*. The brightly spotted tail of the yellow-bellied sea snake may serve to deceive potential predators to strike towards the tail. Studies also suggest that sea snakes may give off a chemical cue that warns away potential generalist predators.

Threats: Boat propeller scars and incidental capture in fishing gear.

Sizing Up Marine Reptiles

Saltwater Crocodile 33 ft (10 m)

Leatherback Sea Turtle 12 ft (3.7 m)

Tourist 6.0 ft (1.8 m)

Green Sea Turtle 4 ft (1.2 m)

Sea Snake 2.5 ft (0.8 m)

Marine Iguana 3.8 ft (1.2 m)

Some Comparative Sizes Amongst Sea Turtles

Olive Ridley Sea Turtle 2.8 ft (0.8 m)

Loggerhead Sea Turtle 3.8 ft (1.2 m)

Leatherback Sea Turtle 12 ft (3.7 m)

Green Sea Turtle 4 ft (1.2 m)

Hawksbill Sea Turtle 3.2 ft (1 m)

The Big Picture:

Sea Turtle Evolution

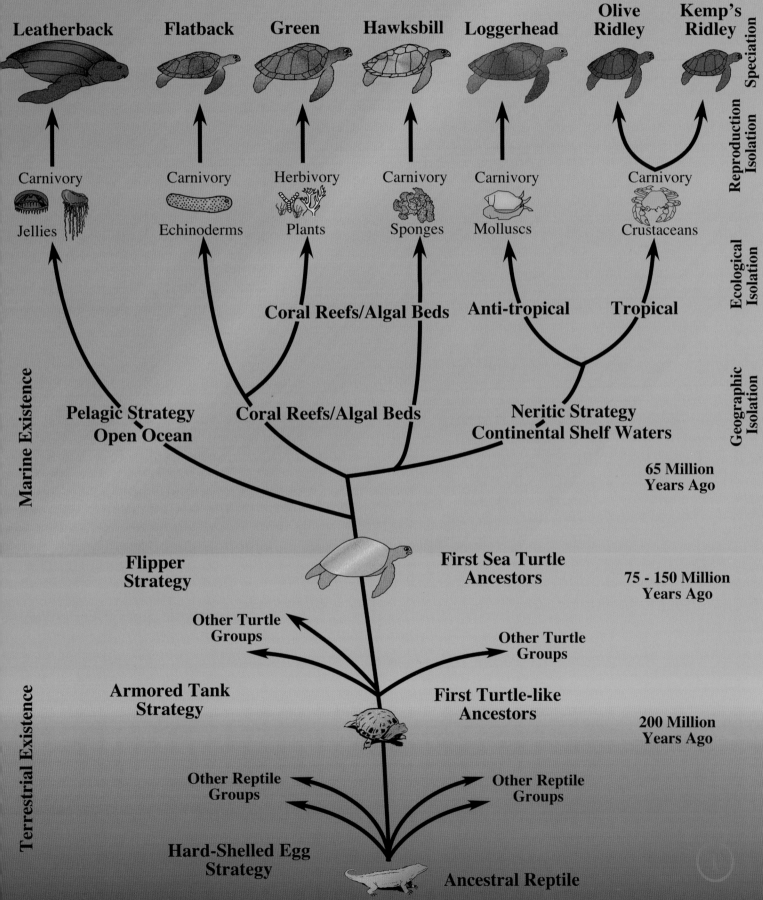

(Modified after Hendrickson, 1980; Dutton *et al*, 1996)

What is a Sea Turtle?

Turtles first appeared on land more than 200 million years ago. Sea turtles originated in the lower Mesozoic Era. The oldest sea turtle fossil is *Santanachelys*, dating back some 112 million years ago to the middle Cretaceous Period. Like marine mammals, sea turtles are thought to have evolved from marsh-dwelling species, which in turn evolved from land-based animals (in this case, land turtles). By the late Cretaceous (around 65 million years ago), four distinct families of sea turtles (Protostegidae, Toxochelidae, Dermochelyidae, Cheloniidae) roamed the world's seas; however, only the latter two families made it into our current era.

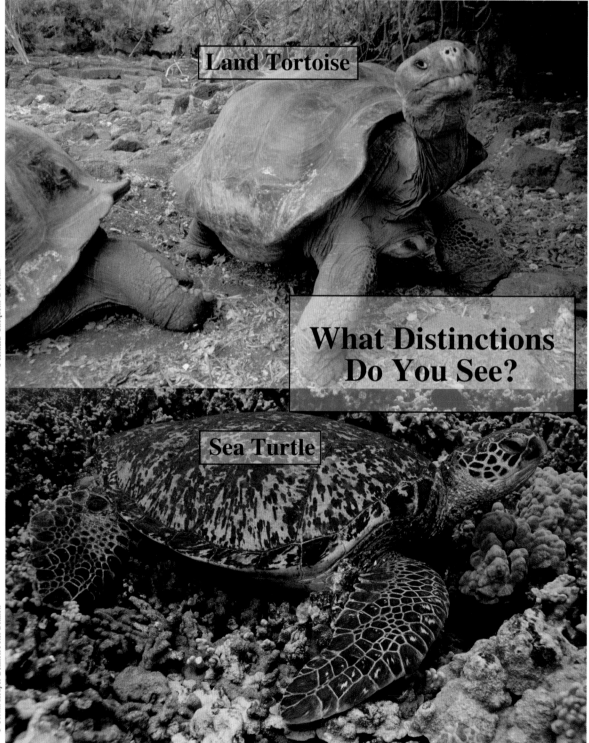

Land Tortoise

What Distinctions Do You See?

Sea Turtle

© Kendra Choquette-D'Avella

© Ursula Keuper-Bennett/Peter Bennett

Tortoises (one group of land turtles) have relatively high-domed shells into which most species can retract their limbs when threatened. Sea turtles have a hydrodynamically-shaped shell for swimming efficiency. Sea turtles cannot retract their head or limbs into their shell for protection and depend on short bursts of speed, deep diving, using the shell as a "shield", and hiding within rocks and crevices for protection.

Tortoises have legs and feet for walking; most are rather slow-moving. (Hey, have you ever tried to run with your hips articulating *inside* your rib cage?) Sea turtles have flippers which act as paddles for swimming and can show great bursts of speed in the water.

Freshwater turtles fall somewhere in-between; they tend to have more flattened, streamlined shells than do their cousins the tortoises, and webbed feet rather than flippers.

Evolution of a Sea Turtle
How In The World Did This Come About?

Over 200 million years ago, terrestrial reptiles lived in an environment full of seriously-toothed predators. It was in such an environment that the first turtle ancestors were thought to have arisen with the advent of an "armored tank" body form. Encasing the majority of the critical organs within a rigid shell proved extremely successful for terrestrial existence (life on land), but it involved a number of critical modifications which would strongly constrain the turtle's return to a marine existence.

To create a hard, box-like body required that the turtle's ribs be flattened and, together with other dermal bone elements, fused together to form a shield (called a "carapace"). Structurally this meant the turtle lost flexibility in its body form. The high domed profile seen in some species may have developed to resist crushing by the jaws of ancient predators. Doming the shell and reducing muscle volume created room for retracting the head and limbs for additional protection, an adaptation eventually used successfully by a wide variety of turtles ranging from high-domed tortoises to nearly flat "softshells".

When turtles returned to the sea, some of these adaptations worked against them ... requiring yet another round of design modification! For starters, a large boxy body form is a lousy swimming shape. Smooth, torpedo-like bodies are better. Consequently, sea turtles typically have a lower profile, shield-like form that is more streamlined and has much less open space inside. Simultaneously, sea turtles needed a means for moving through the water and this meant the development of paddle-like (some would say wing-like) flippers. Enlarged pectoral muscle masses met the challenge of powering a sea turtle through the water, but at the same time they consumed a considerable volume of the chest cavity ... meaning that sea turtles no longer had enough space to retract their head and limbs.

In contrast to the stiffened, elongated forefeet, which moved primarily up and down, the hindfeet and tail now served as elevators and rudders, much like on an airplane. While such adaptations efficiently moved the turtle through an aquatic medium, they proved to be extremely clumsy when moving about on land. Consequently, egg-laying exposed these early marine turtles to a high risk of predation, a reality which surely contributed to the nocturnal nesting habits of most species and a preference for isolated nesting beaches. Finally, repeat nesting patterns and the production of large numbers of eggs evolved as a counter-balance to high rates of mortality in unprotected eggs and hatchlings. The fact that a single female could produce many thousands of eggs over the course of her lifetime eventually ensured the success of the sea turtle's family tree.

The end result was an early form of sea turtle with the following characteristics:

- Relatively large size
- Elongate flipper-like forefeet used for swimming long distances, and out-maneuvering predators, and
- Hindfeet used primarily as a rudder (and for digging nests).

And, while you won't find evidence of these traits in the fossil record, early sea turtles, like their modern-day cousins, were most likely:

- Late-maturing and, for the relative few who reached adulthood, long-lived,
- Highly fecund (they laid large numbers of eggs), balancing high mortality in hatchlings and juveniles, and
- Characterized by external development and no parental care.

It is from this ancestral sea turtle that the existing seven species of sea turtles are thought to have arisen. All living sea turtles share the above characteristics, differing mainly in adaptations related to the primary adult habitat and diet. Such adaptations may decrease competition between species, encouraging low **niche** overlap.

ADAPTATIONS FOR LIVING
IN THE MARINE ENVIRONMENT

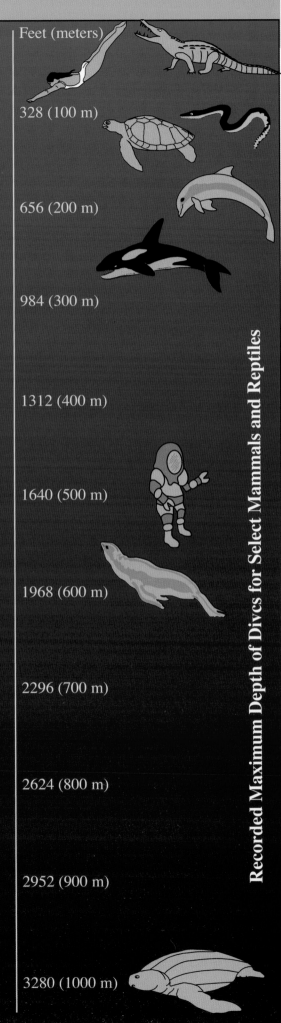

Recorded Maximum Depth of Dives for Select Mammals and Reptiles

Feet (meters)
328 (100 m)
656 (200 m)
984 (300 m)
1312 (400 m)
1640 (500 m)
1968 (600 m)
2296 (700 m)
2624 (800 m)
2952 (900 m)
3280 (1000 m)

So You Want to be a Sea Turtle, Do You?

Water is eight hundred times denser than air, water is a more effective heat sink than air, and sea water contains a large number of dissolved materials that put the "salt" in "saltwater". Animals living in such a medium are exposed to much different pressure, temperature and salinity regimes than their brethren that live on land; thus most marine fish and invertebrates have unique adaptations (fins, gills, etc.) that could never support a terrestrial lifestyle.

Like the dolphin and the seal, sea turtles represent animals that originally were adapted for a terrestrial existence and later returned to a life in the ocean. As a result, several critical adaptations had to occur that required modifying structures once adapted for existence on land.

Breathing: Sea turtles are not fish; they must come to the surface to breathe. Their lungs are adapted for rapid exchange of oxygen, which reduces the amount of time spent at the surface. When making a deep dive, a turtle's lungs are compressed and the residual air is pushed into reinforced trachea that stay open even under the extreme pressures encountered. This effectively pulls the air out of circulation and keeps nitrogen from being forced into the blood (a condition that can lead to "the bends" in SCUBA diving). Even more important with regard to "the bends" (decompression sickness), is that sea turtles store relatively large amounts of oxygen in their blood and muscle tissues rather than in their lungs (see page 21). Because in most species the ribs are fused to their shells, sea turtles can't expand and contract them like you and I in order to draw air into their lungs. Instead, they use the muscles that move their limbs to pump oxygen into their lungs.

Swimming: Sea turtles derive thrust from a powerstroke created by the simultaneous movement of the forelimbs (as opposed to freshwater turtles, which use all of their limbs for propulsion). Their forelimbs have become modified into paddle-like flippers to efficiently move through the water, but this adaptation also makes sea turtles quite inefficient (ok, downright clumsy) when moving on land. Interestingly, a sea turtle uses its rear flippers for propulsion at certain life stages; specifically, the "dog paddle" stroke that characterizes hatchlings and the "rear flipper kick" used by young pelagic-phase sea turtles.

Drinking: All animals need freshwater to survive. Sea turtles are hypoosmotic (compared to seawater), meaning that they tend to lose water to the surrounding ocean. This problem is decreased by their skin and shell being highly resistant to water diffusion and by drinking seawater! Sea turtles have special salt glands (similar to tear ducts), located near the eyes, which constantly pump excess salts out of the body in thick "tears". The tears that people sometimes see in nesting turtles are actually salt secretions from these glands. Salt glands are proportionally much larger in hatchlings than in adults.

Metabolism: Sea turtles have an adjustable metabolism which assists them in staying underwater for long periods of time.

Breath-holding Records

Green turtles – 5 hours

Hawksbills – 45 minutes

Author (DG) - 2 minutes

© Ursula Keuper-Bennett

© Shahin Ansari

The Anatomy of a Sea Turtle

Skull – made-up of fused bones, functions to protect the brain and sensory structures.

Carapace – the dorsal, or upper side, of the shell. In all but the leatherback, the backbone and ribs of the turtle are fused to form the carapace.

Shell – serves to protect internal organs Both the shell and the body in general are tapered to be as hydrodynamic as possible.

Eye

Scute – single **keratinous** scales overlaying the bony carapace. The number and arrangement of the scutes helps to identify one species of sea turtle from another.

Beak – modification of the jaw used for scraping, crushing, tearing or biting.

Cloaca - located beneath the tail.

Rear Flippers - function as rudders for steering, and nest digging.

Mouth – toothless, although green turtles have a serrated beak.

Claw Used for holding onto the female during mating.

Front Flipper Functions both as a wing (lift) and a propeller (thrust)

Plastron – the ventral, or lower side, of the shell. Joined to the **carapace** by cartilage.

© David Schrichte

The Guts of the Matter: A Look at the Major Organ Systems

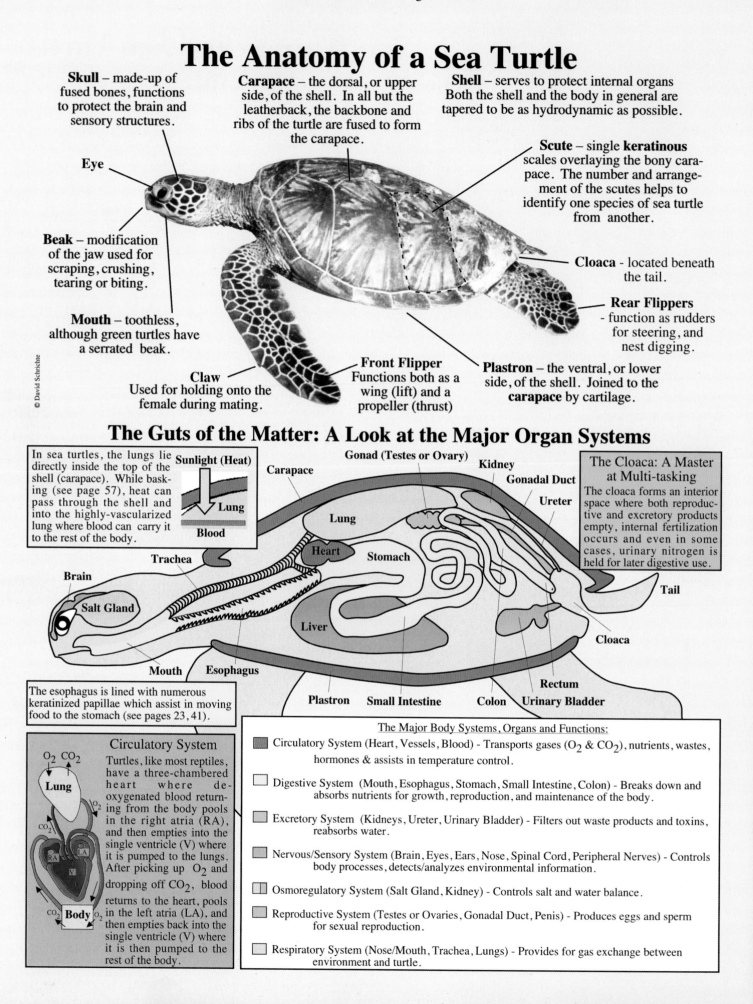

In sea turtles, the lungs lie directly inside the top of the shell (carapace). While basking (see page 57), heat can pass through the shell and into the highly-vascularized lung where blood can carry it to the rest of the body.

Sunlight (Heat)
Lung
Blood

Gonad (Testes or Ovary)
Kidney
Gonadal Duct
Ureter

Carapace

The Cloaca: A Master at Multi-tasking
The cloaca forms an interior space where both reproductive and excretory products empty, internal fertilization occurs and even in some cases, urinary nitrogen is held for later digestive use.

Lung
Heart
Stomach
Trachea
Brain
Salt Gland
Liver
Tail
Cloaca
Mouth
Esophagus
Plastron
Small Intestine
Colon
Rectum
Urinary Bladder

The esophagus is lined with numerous keratinized papillae which assist in moving food to the stomach (see pages 23, 41).

Circulatory System

O_2 CO_2
Lung
O_2
CO_2
CO_2
RA **LA**
V
CO_2 **Body** O_2

Turtles, like most reptiles, have a three-chambered heart where de-oxygenated blood returning from the body pools in the right atria (RA), and then empties into the single ventricle (V) where it is pumped to the lungs. After picking up O_2 and dropping off CO_2, blood returns to the heart, pools in the left atria (LA), and then empties back into the single ventricle (V) where it is then pumped to the rest of the body.

The Major Body Systems, Organs and Functions:

☐ Circulatory System (Heart, Vessels, Blood) - Transports gases (O_2 & CO_2), nutrients, wastes, hormones & assists in temperature control.

☐ Digestive System (Mouth, Esophagus, Stomach, Small Intestine, Colon) - Breaks down and absorbs nutrients for growth, reproduction, and maintenance of the body.

☐ Excretory System (Kidneys, Ureter, Urinary Bladder) - Filters out waste products and toxins, reabsorbs water.

☐ Nervous/Sensory System (Brain, Eyes, Ears, Nose, Spinal Cord, Peripheral Nerves) - Controls body processes, detects/analyzes environmental information.

☐ Osmoregulatory System (Salt Gland, Kidney) - Controls salt and water balance.

☐ Reproductive System (Testes or Ovaries, Gonadal Duct, Penis) - Produces eggs and sperm for sexual reproduction.

☐ Respiratory System (Nose/Mouth, Trachea, Lungs) - Provides for gas exchange between environment and turtle.

What is Thermoregulation?

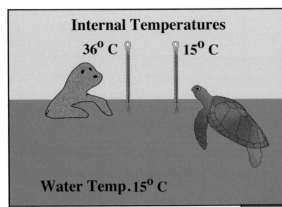

Internal Temperatures
36° C   15° C

Water Temp. 15° C

**North Temperate Water
(Pacific Northwest near Seattle)**

Internal Temperatures
36° C   30° C

Water Temp. 30° C

**Sub-Tropical Water
(near Baja, California, Mexico)**

Basking behavior (whether at the water surface or on a beach) is thought to play a role in thermoregulation (see pages 55 - 56). Some sea turtles may function as regional endotherms; that is, they keep only their active tissues (and not the entire body) at an elevated temperature. Such an adaptation is possible due to the heat lag associated with the large body size of many sea turtles and the excellent insulatory capabilities of some of their tissues. By elevating the temperature of their pectoral muscles above that of the surrounding water, the turtle's ability to sustain swimming over long periods is increased and may help to account for the ability of these animals to make long distance migrations.

Most sea turtles that are exposed to cold water for extended periods become cold-stunned, a condition that can be fatal and is most often documented when an affected animal is immobilized and "strands" (beaches) itself along the coast. Some sea turtles, including the East Pacific green turtle, will over-winter; that is, they will lie motionless at depth when winter winds and surface waters become inhospitable. Other sea turtles in temperate climates will actually bury most of their body in soft sediments to help insulate against heat loss.

Some sea turtle species may spend hours floating on the surface; in essence, an aquatic form of **basking**, allowing the turtle to absorb solar heat energy ... and providing a welcome footrest for ocean-going seabirds.

Question: What reasons can you give for why sea turtles don't lay their eggs in the water?

© Robert L. Pitman

© Robert Thorn

Mechanisms for Thermoregulation

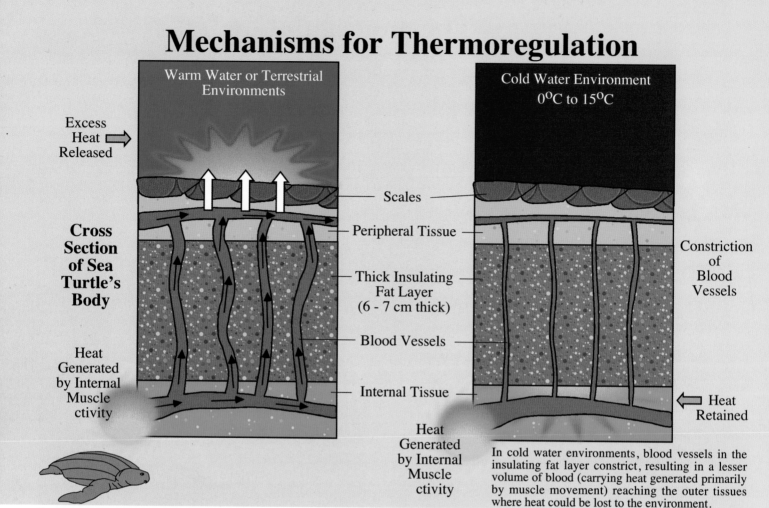

Warm Water or Terrestrial Environments

Cold Water Environment
0°C to 15°C

Excess Heat Released

Cross Section of Sea Turtle's Body

Heat Generated by Internal Muscle ctivity

Scales

Peripheral Tissue

Thick Insulating Fat Layer (6 - 7 cm thick)

Blood Vessels

Internal Tissue

Constriction of Blood Vessels

Heat Retained

Heat Generated by Internal Muscle ctivity

In cold water environments, blood vessels in the insulating fat layer constrict, resulting in a lesser volume of blood (carrying heat generated primarily by muscle movement) reaching the outer tissues where heat could be lost to the environment.

Large size translates to a low surface area (height x length) to volume (height x length x width) ratio; minimizing external area relative to their mass contributes to maintenance of internal core temperatures.

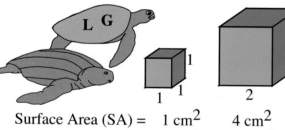

Some species will hibernate in channel mud when temperatures go too low. The mud serves to insulate the turtle.

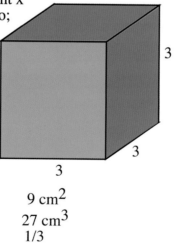

Surface Area (SA) =	1 cm^2	4 cm^2	9 cm^2
Volume (V) =	1 cm^3	8 cm^3	27 cm^3
Ratio = (SA/V) =	1	1/2	1/3

The end result of this basic physics lesson is that large adult turtles have a better ability to retain heat than smaller ones because more of their internal area is not adjacent to their outside surfaces (which translates to lower relative heat loss).

? Brrrrr!!!

Many species will migrate to warmer waters when temperatures in winter drop below 15°C. Leatherbacks are a special case. Due to their large size and exceptional heat capacity, they can live in very cold water, even venturing into subartic zones to feed on jellyfish and other delicacies.

Holding Your Breath: How Sea Turtles Breath Air & Stay Underwater

Certain sea turtle species are breath holding champions!

In regards to the structure of their respiratory system, sea turtles may more closely resemble marine mammals than they do other reptiles.

Sea turtles have the highest oxygen consumption rate of any reptile.

Sea turtles store high amounts of oxygen in blood and muscle tissue.

Adult leatherback sea turtles can dive deeply, holding their breath, for up to 70 minutes!

Loggerhead sea turtles have been known to survive for hours under anoxic (lacking oxygen) conditions, such an adaptation may assist in overwintering and hibernation activities.

Sea turtles appear to be extremely efficient at buffering the carbon dioxide in their blood, minimizing the effect of CO_2 build-up within their body systems.

A sea turtle's lung provides more area for gas exchange then other reptiles.

All sea turtles have multi-chambered lungs full of spongy and elastic tissue providing large amounts of surface area for oxygen and carbon dioxide exchange; this allows sea turtles to exchange oxygen at a faster rate than any other reptile. Sea turtles also have a strongly reinforced airway which is thought to help prevent airway collapse from the increased pressures encountered during deep diving. Sea turtles breathe by moving their pectoral and pelvic muscles (think of flapping your arms and legs), which compresses the area containing the lungs and changes the pressure within the lung cavity allowing both inhalation and exhalation to occur.

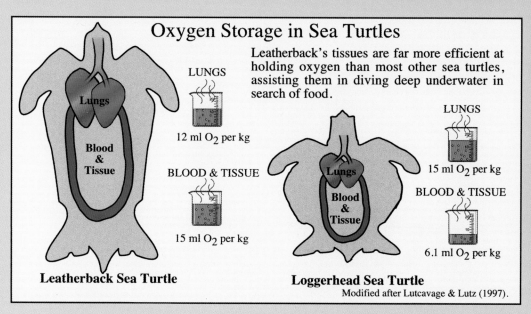

Oxygen Storage in Sea Turtles

Leatherback's tissues are far more efficient at holding oxygen than most other sea turtles, assisting them in diving deep underwater in search of food.

Leatherback Sea Turtle

LUNGS — 12 ml O$_2$ per kg

BLOOD & TISSUE — 15 ml O$_2$ per kg

Loggerhead Sea Turtle

LUNGS — 15 ml O$_2$ per kg

BLOOD & TISSUE — 6.1 ml O$_2$ per kg

Modified after Lutcavage & Lutz (1997).

Shallow diving, air-breathing organisms usually inhale before a dive and store most of the oxygen for that dive within their lungs. In contrast, the leatherback sea turtle is adapted to store much of the oxygen it needs for deep-diving within its blood and other tissues. This has the advantage of making oxygen more quickly available to the body cells and keeping it available even after lung collapse associated with a deep dive would normally have cut off those oxygen stores.

Flying Through the Water: The Wonders of Sea Turtle Locomotion

The angling of the forelimb as the limb goes up and down, results in the lift force being directed forward as propulsion.

© David L. Schrichte

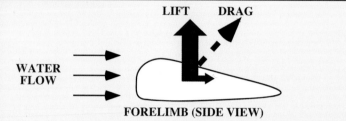

FORELIMB (SIDE VIEW)

Lift results from differences in pressure as a medium (air or water) flows across a foil (hydrofoil or aerofoil (a wing)). Because lift is generated perpendicular to flow, when a turtle is gliding lift helps to keep it in the water column; when flapping its flippers (powerstroking), the lift produced is translated to thrust.

The Wing

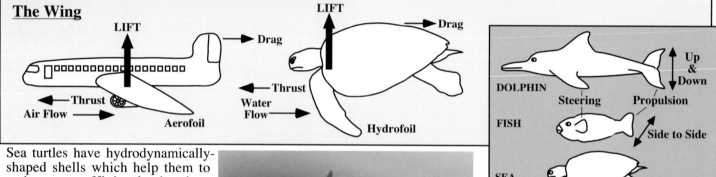

Sea turtles have hydrodynamically-shaped shells which help them to swim more efficiently, but into which they can no longer retract for protection; as a result, most sea turtles depend more on short bursts of speed and hiding within rocks and crevices for protection. Additionally, the shells are often lighter than those of land tortoises, helping them to avoid sinking while in the water and allowing them to swim more efficiently.

© Ursula Keuper-Bennett/Peter Bennett

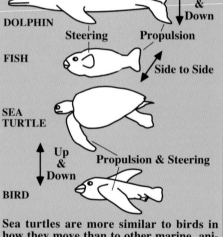

Sea turtles are more similar to birds in how they move than to other marine animals such as fish or dolphins

The Engine

To provide for propulsion, a large section of the chest cavity is taken up by pectoral muscles. Contraction of these muscles also assists in bringing about inhalation and exhalation of the lungs.

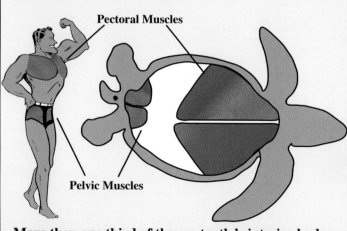

Pectoral Muscles

Pelvic Muscles

More than one third of the sea turtle's interior body cavity area is taken up by the pectoral muscles!

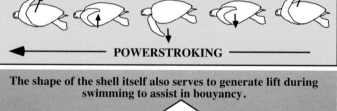

POWERSTROKING

The shape of the shell itself also serves to generate lift during swimming to assist in bouyancy.

Lift

Thrust

Ursula Keuper-Bennett/Peter Bennett

The Problem of Salt Regulation
(Or How An Aquatic Turtle Can Die of Thirst)

Reptiles have body fluids (blood, interstitial, etc.) that are far less salty than sea water. Without special modifications, a turtle that finds itself underwater in the sea runs the risk of dehydration. This is because water will move from areas of high to low concentration; in seawater, such animals will lose water from their bodies to the surrounding salty ocean. Water is replaced by drinking more sea water, which in turn raises the saltiness of the body with respect to the sea. Under such a situation there can be no net gain of freshwater unless the salts are excreted in a solution at least as concentrated as that of seawater. The result is that without some mechanism to get rid of the salts, sea turtles would become dehydrated, even though they are surrounded by water. Like other reptiles adapted to live in the ocean, sea turtles have special adaptations to minimize salt gain and water loss.

A Basic Primer on Diffusion & Osmosis

Diffusion

Relative Equilibrium

A → B   A | B

Given two bodies of freshwater, separated by a permeable membrane, water will flow across the membrane until the two bodies reach a state of equilibrium where the water is evenly dispersed. At this point, individual water molecules will still move, but there is no longer a concentration gradient, and therefore diffusion ceases.

Osmosis

Relative Equilibrium

A → B   A | B

Now if those two bodies of water (say the blood of a turtle and the ocean, separated by the semipermeable skin of the turtle) contained various concentrations of elements (salts) which cannot cross the semipermeable membrane, water will flow across the membrane from the area of lower salt concentration in order for the two bodies to reach a state of relative equilibrium.

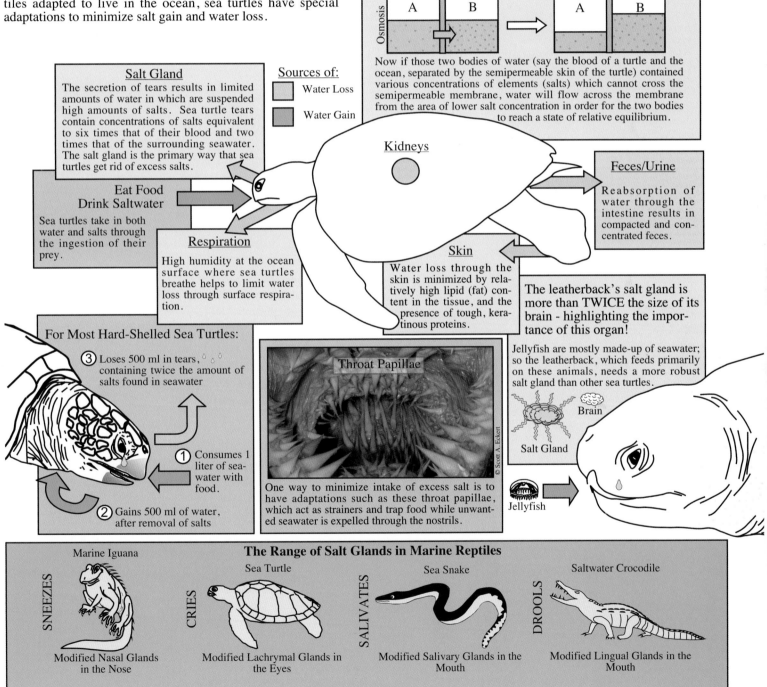

Sources of:
- Water Loss
- Water Gain

Salt Gland
The secretion of tears results in limited amounts of water in which are suspended high amounts of salts. Sea turtle tears contain concentrations of salts equivalent to six times that of their blood and two times that of the surrounding seawater. The salt gland is the primary way that sea turtles get rid of excess salts.

Eat Food / Drink Saltwater
Sea turtles take in both water and salts through the ingestion of their prey.

Respiration
High humidity at the ocean surface where sea turtles breathe helps to limit water loss through surface respiration.

Kidneys

Feces/Urine
Reabsorption of water through the intestine results in compacted and concentrated feces.

Skin
Water loss through the skin is minimized by relatively high lipid (fat) content in the tissue, and the presence of tough, keratinous proteins.

The leatherback's salt gland is more than TWICE the size of its brain - highlighting the importance of this organ!

Jellyfish are mostly made-up of seawater; so the leatherback, which feeds primarily on these animals, needs a more robust salt gland than other sea turtles.

Brain

Salt Gland

Jellyfish

For Most Hard-Shelled Sea Turtles:

③ Loses 500 ml in tears, containing twice the amount of salts found in seawater

① Consumes 1 liter of seawater with food.

② Gains 500 ml of water, after removal of salts

Throat Papillae
One way to minimize intake of excess salt is to have adaptations such as these throat papillae, which act as strainers and trap food while unwanted seawater is expelled through the nostrils.

© Scott A. Eckert

The Range of Salt Glands in Marine Reptiles

Marine Iguana	Sea Turtle	Sea Snake	Saltwater Crocodile
SNEEZES	**CRIES**	**SALIVATES**	**DROOLS**
Modified Nasal Glands in the Nose	Modified Lachrymal Glands in the Eyes	Modified Salivary Glands in the Mouth	Modified Lingual Glands in the Mouth

Senses

Vision: Sea turtles are thought to be nearsighted above water. Loggerhead and green sea turtles have been shown to see all colors (from "long wavelength" reds through to "short wavelength" blues); however, they see orange best!

Hearing: No external ears, ear canals are covered by skin. Sea turtles are sensitive to low frequency sound up to 1000 hz.

Smell: Acute sense of smell, may serve to allow for prey detection in murky water.

Magnetism: Can sense the direction of the earth's magnetic field and also distinguish among magnetic fields characteristic of different geographic areas.

Navigation: A wide range of theories have been suggested to account for the ability of some sea turtles to migrate through thousands of miles of open ocean, from feeding areas to nesting grounds. Many lines of evidence suggest that adult sea turtles will return to lay their eggs on or near the same beaches they emerged from as hatchlings. Some say that hatchlings taste the water upon first entering the sea, creating a unique memory of the chemical "fingerprint" of their nesting waters which they then use twenty or so years later to find their way home. Another idea is that turtles "imprint" on the unique magnetic field of their home beach and use this information to navigate back. Still others theorize that turtles navigate by the stars or the sun, oceanic temperatures or currents, geologic features, or by using patterns of ocean waves. Many sea turtles have been found to have a substance called **magnetite** in small amounts within their brains; this same substance has been found within the brains of homing animals like pigeons and may explain how turtles can sense the earth's magnetic field. The answer to precisely how turtles navigate is probably that they use a variety of cues and that the particular suite chosen may depend upon both the life history stage and the cues that are available where the turtle lives.

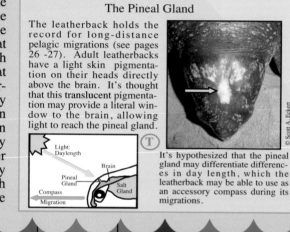

The Pineal Gland

The leatherback holds the record for long-distance pelagic migrations (see pages 26-27). Adult leatherbacks have a light skin pigmentation on their heads directly above the brain. It's thought that this translucent pigmentation may provide a literal window to the brain, allowing light to reach the pineal gland.

It's hypothesized that the pineal gland may differentiate differences in day length, which the leatherback may be able to use as an accessory compass during its migrations.

© Scott A. Eckert

0 — Red — Orange — Yellow — Green — Blue — indigo — Violet — 0

Meters
10 — 33
20 — 66
30 — 98
40

Feet

A Little Insight on our View of the Vision Thing...

In evolving for a lifetime spent virtually entirely underwater, the sea turtles have modified their visual systems from those possessed by their terrestrial and freshwater turtle relatives. Cutting edge research shows that while they are still capable of seeing light throughout the visible spectrum (from "long wavelength" reds through to "short wavelength" blues), they have shifted both their daytime and nighttime sensitivity towards the greenish hues that predominate in the ocean environment. In fact, while land-based turtles are much more sensitive to red and yellow lights, sea turtle sensitivity is actually very similar to our own visual abilities. Sea turtles probably also share our well-developed ability to discriminate colors. However, unlike humans and non-marine turtles, sea turtles do not see particularly clearly on land. Consequently, sea turtles probably find things quite blurry above water, just as we humans require goggles to correct for what would otherwise be a very blurry landscape under water!

What's in a Name?

SEA TURTLES OF THE WORLD

There are seven recognized species of sea turtles living in the world's oceans today.

© Scott A. Eckert

Green sea turtle

Popularly believed to have been named for the greenish tinge of its internal fat, which may absorb green pigments (color) from the plants the turtle consumes.

Hawksbill sea turtle

Named for its relatively narrow head and the bird-like shape of its beak. The generic name *Eretmochelys* means "oar turtle". The specific name *imbricata* refers to the over-lapping nature of the carapace **scutes**.

© Ursula Keuper-Bennett/Peter Bennett

© Scott A. Eckert

Leatherback sea turtle

Named for its tough rubber-like skin and lack of a fused bony shell. The generic name *Dermochelys* refers to the distinctive leathery, scaleless skin of the adult turtle.

Loggerhead sea turtle

Named for its relatively massive, block-like head. The generic name *Caretta* is a latinized version of the French word "caret", meaning turtle, tortoise, or sea turtle.

© Scott A. Eckert

© Ursula Keuper-Bennett/Peter Bennett

Kemp's ridley sea turtle

Named after Richard Kemp, who helped discover the species. The term "ridley" may refer to a 'riddler', as scientists once had difficulty deter-mining where these animals originat-ed or nested.

© Scott A. Eckert

Olive ridley sea turtle

Perhaps named for the olive-green color of its shell. *Lepidochelys* comes from a Greek root meaning "scaly"; the olive ridley has the greatest number of "shell scales" (**scutes**) of any of the sea turtles.

Flatback sea turtle

`C'mon, one guess...

© P. C. H. Pritchard

Leatherback Sea Turtles (*Dermochelys coriacea*)

Description: Largest of all turtles, adult males can exceed nine feet in length and weigh 2000 lbs. or more. There is a difference in size between Atlantic and Pacific populations, with Pacific leatherbacks being the smaller of the two. **Carapace** color ranges from black to dark brown, often with pink, white or bluish splotches. Plastron is whitish, giving the animal a counter-shading effect. The **carapace** is elongated and has seven narrow ridges running its entire length, with six longitudinal ridges found on the **plastron**. Scientists believe that the ridges along their backs improve laminar flow and promote swimming efficiency.

Adults lack head and flipper scales and have three interlocking cusps for slicing into prey. Unlike other sea turtle species, leatherbacks lack a hard shell; the carapace is composed of small osteodermic pieces (think tiny little bones) embedded in a thick matrix of cartilaginous dermal tissue; as such, there are no scutes present on the shell. Leatherbacks have no claws on their flippers, which are more elongated and paddle-like than in other sea turtles.

Distribution: Found worldwide in all oceans, from Nova Scotia and Alaska south to South Africa and New Zealand. Leatherbacks have been found in the Barents Sea, making them the most northern-occurring reptile (whether aquatic or terrestrial) in the world. Leatherbacks have even been seen swimming amongst ice!

Nesting: Nesting seasons vary strongly depending upon geographic location. Nesting sites tend to be located on isolated beaches adjacent to deep water (i.e. no reefs for these large, easily injured animals to cross). Females mate every two to three (or more) years and can nest as often as 12 times during a reproductive year! The comparatively large eggs average about 2" in diameter.

© Scott A. Eckert

© Scott A. Eckert

CRITICALLY ENDANGERED ▬ **ENDANGERED**

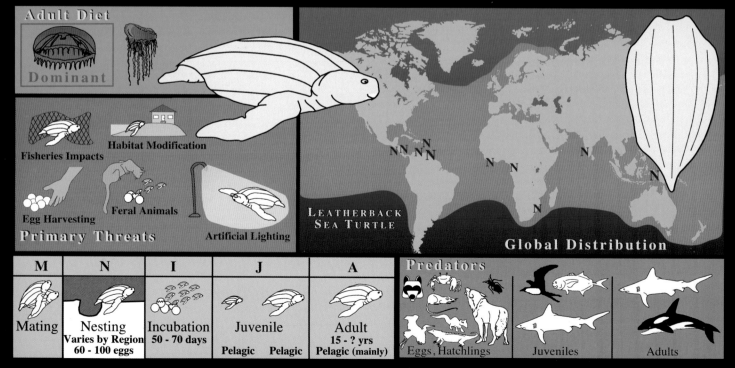

Adult Diet — Dominant

Primary Threats: Fisheries Impacts, Habitat Modification, Egg Harvesting, Feral Animals, Artificial Lighting

LEATHERBACK SEA TURTLE — **Global Distribution**

M	N	I	J	A
Mating	Nesting — Varies by Region — 60 - 100 eggs	Incubation — 50 - 70 days	Juvenile — Pelagic — Pelagic	Adult — 15 - ? yrs — Pelagic (mainly)

Predators

| Eggs, Hatchlings | Juveniles | Adults |

Ecology. Leatherbacks can dive deeper than 3900 feet (1200 m). Such deep diving may be possible in part due to a flexible carapace and plastron (made of cartilage embedded with miniature bones) that resist cracking under pressure at depth. Additionally, deep diving may be facilitated by the ability of both the leatherback's blood and muscle tissue to hold high amounts of oxygen (rather than storing oxygen in the lungs), because during deep dives the lungs would be strongly compressed by the increased water pressure .

Primarily pelagic, the leatherback has the widest range of any sea turtle and tolerates cold water due to thermoregulatory adaptations (see page 19 - 20). Mechanisms for thermoregulation include counter-current heat exchange systems in the circulatory apparatus in their limbs, high oil content and large body size.

Diet: Leatherbacks feed exclusively on soft-bodied pelagic prey such as sea jellies and salps. The throat is lined with stiff spines to assist in swallowing of prey (see page 41). Though primarily solitary, leatherbacks may gather in small groups in areas where their prey are concentrated.

This map illustrates the movements, over the course of nearly 2 years in some cases, of adult females departing nesting beaches in Mexico and Trinidad and returning to high seas foraging grounds. Leatherbacks swim some 10,000 miles per year, making them one of the most migratory species on earth. Remote sensing technologies not only reveal fascinating ecological aspects, but also assist government and industry in developing strategies to reduce interaction between endangered sea turtles and high seas fishing fleets.

With the development of high-tech instruments, such as satellite transmitters, and their application to leatherback sea turtles pioneered by Dr. Scott Eckert (WIDECAST) and his colleagues, we are learning more about leatherbacks than could have been imagined even a decade ago.

Population Status: Today this elusive and magnificent species, which has plied the oceans since before the Age of Dinosaurs, is classified by international authorities as "critically endangered" throughout its range. Some of the largest nesting assemblages have virtually collapsed in recent years. For example, the nesting population in Malaysia represents 1% of what it was in the 1950's, due largely to decades of unregulated egg harvest. The Pacific coast of Mexico, until recently the species' largest nesting colony, is today less than 10% of what it was just a decade ago, due largely to the incidental capture and mortality of sub-adults and adults in fishing gear on foraging grounds far distant from the nesting beaches.

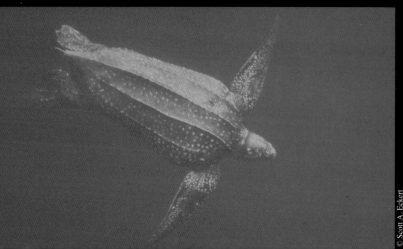

In tropical deep water habitat, there is an ancient rhythm to a leatherback's day. During early morning, the huge turtles dive to depths following the downward migrations of their prey, sea jellies and plankton, which often will retreat to deeper depths away from the light of day.

Around mid-day, when the majority of their prey have sunk to depths where the energy gained by feeding isn't compensated by the energy costs of diving to such depths, leatherbacks typically travel, just below the surface, between foraging grounds. Occasional very deep dives may be for predator avoidance.

During the night, leatherbacks feed on their prey, sea jellies and plankton, in the tropical surface waters.

Leatherback Diving Cycles

Loggerhead Sea Turtles
(*Caretta caretta*)

Description: Adult size varies geographically, with Western Atlantic residents averaging about 250 lbs. and attaining weights of 400 lbs. or more, and Mediterranean residents rarely exceeding 200 lbs. Typical adult **carapace** length ranges from 30 - 42 inches. The relatively large head is diagnostic, and it supports powerful jaw muscles that enable this turtle to effectively feed on hard-shelled prey. The carapace is slightly heart-shaped, the **scutes** do not overlap one another, and the nuchal **scute** is in direct contact with the first costal **scute** on each side. Carapace color is reddish-brown, while the plastron is generally a creamy yellow color. The posterior portion of the carapace is thickest; given its relatively slow swimming speed when compared

© Scott A. Eckert

to other sea turtles, this may provide for additional protection against shark predation. Each limb bears two claws. More than 50 species of invertebrates (such as barnacles, tunicates, sponges, and crabs) have been found associated with the loggerhead's shell!

Nesting: In Florida, one of the largest nesting grounds in the world, mating tends to occur between March and June. After mating, males do not stick around while the females nest; instead the males tend to return to resident foraging grounds. As in other sea turtle species, females are highly fecund and can nest from three to five times, sometimes more, within a single nesting season. Nesting does not typically occur annually because a female needs time to replenish her strength before she is adequately prepared to enter into another breeding season. Major nesting areas include Masirah Island off Oman and the east coast of Florida (USA).

© David Schrichte

⊕ ENDANGERED ▬ THREATENED

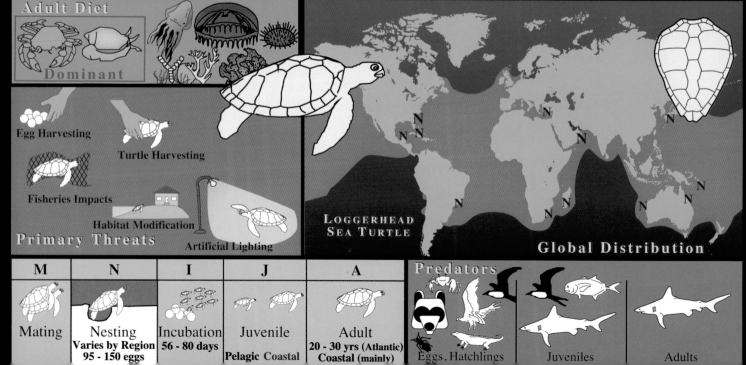

Adult Diet
Dominant

Egg Harvesting

Turtle Harvesting

Fisheries Impacts

Habitat Modification

Artificial Lighting

Primary Threats

LOGGERHEAD
SEA TURTLE

Global Distribution

Predators

M	N	I	J	A
Mating	Nesting **Varies by Region 95 - 150 eggs**	Incubation 56 - 80 days	Juvenile **Pelagic Coastal**	Adult 20 - 30 yrs (Atlantic) **Coastal (mainly)**

Eggs, Hatchlings | Juveniles | Adults

7,500 Miles!
(12,000 Kilometers!)

Japan
Nesting Beaches

Mexico
Feeding Areas

© Scott A. Eckert

© Scott A. Eckert

© Scott A. Eckert

Hatchlings are born with three keels running the length of the **carapace**, but these keels tend to disappear as the turtles grow. Growth rate is highly dependant upon temperature, as well as food quality and quantity. Hatchlings in the southeastern U.S. are thought to enter oceanic driftlines composed primarily of the brown seaweed *Sargassum*, and from there are carried passively on the North Atlantic subtropical gyre to the eastern North Atlantic, including the Azores. After several years of **pelagic** existence, juveniles, typically 20-25 inches in shell length, return or are returned by currents to the western North Atlantic to become resident **benthic** feeders on the continental shelf.

Population Status: Though listed as a **Threatened Species** under the U. S. Endangered Species Act, concern exists that populations nesting north of Florida have declined dramatically and may warrant endangered status. Once thriving populations elsewhere in the world are also declining, including in Australia where incidental capture in trawl nets is a serious management concern.

Distribution: Loggerheads are found as far north as Newfoundland and northern Europe and as far south as Argentina, but they have a predominately temperate nesting distribution. They are able to tolerate lower water temperatures than most other sea turtles, with the exception of the leatherback. They are found in coastal, estuarine, and continental shelf waters both in the tropics and subtropics, but undertake transoceanic journeys as young juveniles. For example, recent satellite tagging data (see page 105) has shown that Pacific loggerheads migrate over 7,500 miles (12,000 km) between nesting beaches in Japan and their feeding grounds off the coast of Mexico. Taking up to six years to make the journey, hatchlings leave the natal beaches of Japan and work their way across the Pacific to rich feeding grounds off the coast of Mexico. Later, as adults, they make the return journey in order to mate and nest.

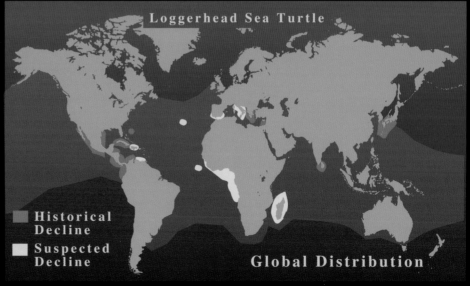

Loggerhead Sea Turtle

Historical Decline

Suspected Decline

Global Distribution

After Table 1 in NMFS 1990.

Green Sea Turtles (*Chelonia mydas*)

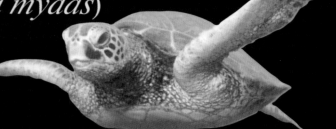

© Ursula Keuper-Bennett/Peter Bennett

Description: The average length and weight of adults varies geographically. The typical adult boasts a carapace some 40 inches in length and a weight of 200 – 500 lbs., making this species the largest of the hard-shelled sea turtles. **Carapace** color ranges from olive brown to black (especially with East Pacific populations), the **scutes** are non-overlapping, and the **plastron** is yellowish. Each flipper contains a single claw. Unlike other sea turtle species, greens have only a single pair of prefrontal scales between their eyes. Green sea turtles are most often found near continental coasts and oceanic islands between 30° north and 30° south, with most of the nesting habitat lying within tropical seas. Green sea turtles nest in more than 80 countries worldwide, and may forage in the coastal waters of more than 140 countries!

Diet: Along with manatees and dugongs, green sea turtles are the largest of the grazing marine herbivores (see pages 40 and 42). In some areas the diet is composed nearly entirely of seagrass, such as in the Caribbean where *Thalassia testudinum* grows in lush meadows and is commonly referred to as "turtle grass"! In contrast, sea weeds and algae are often the daily special for Pacific populations.

Hawaiian Islands where the majority of mating and nesting occurs. Hawaiian green turtles aren't the record holders in the long distance migration contest for this species, however; that title is held by a population of green turtles that feeds in the coastal waters of Brazil and migrates over 1400 miles to Ascension Island (in the middle of the Atlantic Ocean) for mating and nesting.

Most nests are laid in open sandy beach habitat, with the female forming a distinctive "body pit" 2 to 3 feet in width and depth. Nesting may take 2 hours or more, resulting in a typical **clutch** of 75 to 150 eggs. Females have an inter-nesting interval of 12 to 15 days, depositing multiple nests during a single reproductive season. Individual females do not breed every year, but return faithfully to their chosen nesting grounds every 2-5 (or more) years.

© Kendra Choquette-D'Avella

Nesting: It's difficult to generalize with a globally distributed species, but, as an example, between May and August in Hawai'i, adult green turtles undergo a long journey from their feeding grounds in the Main Hawaiian Islands to French Frigate Shoals in the Northwestern

© Ursula Keuper-Bennett/Peter Bennett

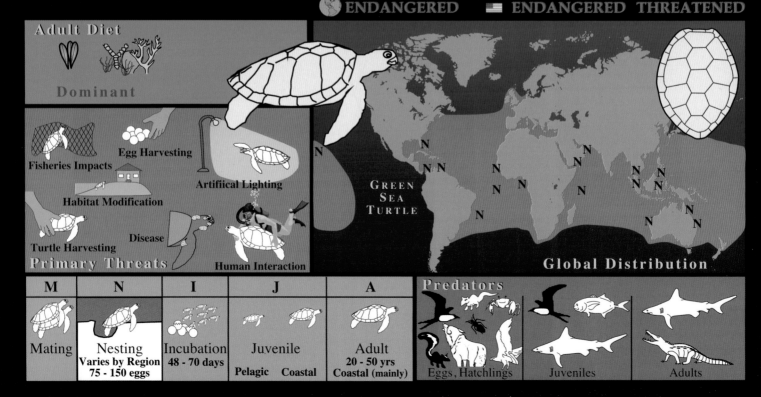

ENDANGERED ≡ ENDANGERED THREATENED

Adult Diet

Dominant

Fisheries Impacts
Egg Harvesting
Artifiical Lighting
Habitat Modification
Disease
Turtle Harvesting
Human Interaction
Primary Threats

GREEN SEA TURTLE

N N N N N N N N N N N N N N N N N N N

Global Distribution

M	N	I	J	A
Mating	Nesting Varies by Region 75 - 150 eggs	Incubation 48 - 70 days	Juvenile Pelagic Coastal	Adult 20 - 50 yrs Coastal (mainly)

Predators

Eggs, Hatchlings	Juveniles	Adults

East Pacific Green Sea Turtles (*Chelonia mydas*)

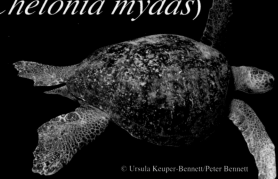

© Ursula Keuper-Bennett/Peter Bennett

Description: The East Pacific green sea turtle is smaller, darker in coloration, and has a differently-shaped carapace than other green sea turtles. Shell length is about 32 inches. Some experts consider the East Pacific greens, often called "black turtles", to be a separate species (*Chelonia agassizii*).

© Ursula Keuper-Bennett/Peter Bennett

Distribution: Adults inhabit bays and protected shorelines from southern California (USA) to Chile, although wayward individuals are reported as far north as Alaska and as far west as Hawai'i and Japan. Most nesting occurs in Mexico, Central America and the Galapagos Islands. In some areas, they share nesting beaches with leatherbacks and olive ridleys. The black turtles tend to nest higher above the tidal line at slightly different times of the year; such an adaptation may serve to limit competition over prime nesting space between sea turtle species.

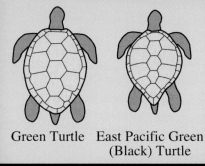

Green Turtle   East Pacific Green (Black) Turtle

Diet: Like the green turtle, the black turtle is primarily vegetarian as an adult, feeding on seagrasses, algae and possibly mangrove shoots. There is evidence, however, that small fish, as well as molluscs (primarily sea slugs), polychaetes (marine worms), jellyfish, sponges, amphipods and other invertebrates are also eaten.

Threats: The once thriving Mexican colony has been decimated due in large part to an active turtle fishery that operated from the 1960s through the mid-1980s. Today an ongoing but entirely illegal harvest (of both eggs and turtles) is the largest threat to black turtles throughout their range, followed closely by incidental catch in nearshore artisanal set-net fisheries.

The southern black sea turtle population may be under increased pressure from the recent explosion of coastal fishing activity in the Galapagos Archipelago. Currently, only Galapagos Islanders are legally allowed to take these turtles on a subsistence basis and under extreme circumstances.

Male   Female

© P. C. H. Pritchard

⊛ENDANGERED ▤ENDANGERED

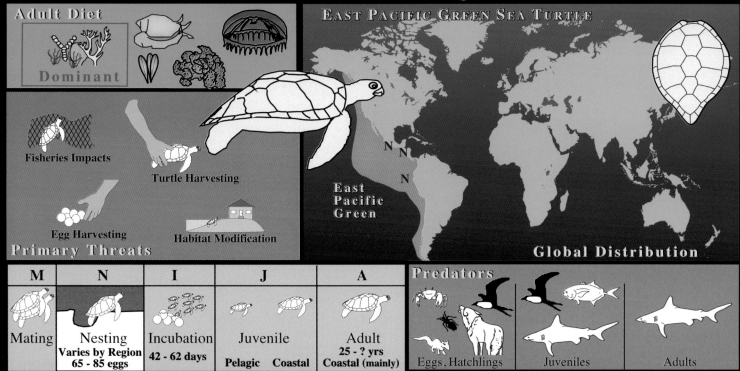

Adult Diet

Dominant

Primary Threats

Fisheries Impacts

Turtle Harvesting

Egg Harvesting

Habitat Modification

EAST PACIFIC GREEN SEA TURTLE

East Pacific Green

Global Distribution

M	N	I	J	A
Mating	Nesting **Varies by Region 65 - 85 eggs**	Incubation **42 - 62 days**	Juvenile **Pelagic Coastal**	Adult **25 - ? yrs Coastal (mainly)**

Predators

| Eggs, Hatchlings | Juveniles | Adults |

Hawksbill Sea Turtles (*Eretmochelys imbricata*)

Description: Adults weigh in at 60 to nearly 200 pounds, averaging 100-150 lbs. Shell length typically ranges from 25 to 35 inches throughout the species' global range, making it the smallest of the sea turtles, with the exception of the ridleys. The "hawksbill" gets its common name (in English, anyway) from its narrow face and bird-like beak. **Carapace** color is "tortoiseshell", ranging from golden to dark brown with red, black and orange streaks. The posterior (rear) edge is serrated, especially in young animals, and the scutes overlap one another like shingles on a roof. Each flipper usually bears two claws. Hawksbills are the most tropical of the sea turtles, often associated with healthy coral reefs.

Diet: Hawksbills specialize on sponges (obligate **spongivores**), with comparatively minor contributions by other benthic invertebrates. Remarkably, scientists are finding that even when surrounded by dozens of species of sponge, the hawksbill will preferentially feed on only a handful of species, showing an unusual and highly refined dietary specificity (see page 43). The hooked beak of this animal is well-adapted for probing into holes and crevices in search of its prey.

© Ursula Keuper-Bennett/Peter Bennett

Nesting: Hawksbill nesting under U. S. jurisdiction includes both Caribbean and Pacific holdings and, as is true throughout its global range, the small size and agility of this animal allows it to climb onto rockier coastlines than other sea turtles in search of nesting beaches. The species has declined dramatically in many places, resulting in fewer females returning to their nesting beaches. In some ways the resulting patterns of dispersed and low density nesting, coupled with the species' penchant for placing its nests in obscure sites amongst the beach vegetation, may account for its survival into the 21st century.

In general, nestings occur at 14 - 16 day intervals; females do not tend to nest in consecutive years. The eggs are small, about the size of ping-pong balls, and 200 or more may be laid at one time.

© Kendra Choquette D'Avella

Adult Diet

Dominant

Primary Threats

Fisheries Impacts

Habitat Modification

Turtle Harvesting/Shell Products

Egg Harvesting

Feral/Exotic Animals

Artificial Lighting

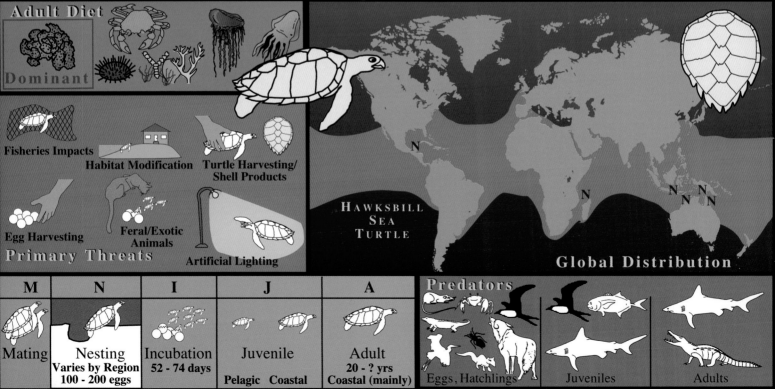

CRITICALLY ENDANGERED ENDANGERED

HAWKSBILL SEA TURTLE

N   N   N N N

Global Distribution

Predators

Eggs, Hatchlings   Juveniles   Adults

M	N	I	J	A
Mating	Nesting **Varies by Region 100 - 200 eggs**	Incubation **52 - 74 days**	Juvenile **Pelagic Coastal**	Adult **20 - ? yrs Coastal (mainly)**

© Kendra Choquette-D'Avella

© Kendra Choquette-D'Avella

© Kendra Choquette-D'Avella

Chelonitoxin refers to a form of poisoning that occurs from humans eating sea turtles. Perhaps in the case of the hawksbill it results from toxins associated with sponges that the turtle feeds on, toxins that "bioaccumulate" within its tissues. Effects from consuming hawksbill meat include headaches, nausea, vomiting, rapid heartbeat, pale skin, severe stomach pain, sweating, dizziness, difficulty in swallowing, skin rash, and a burning sensation around the mouth, lips and tongue. In severe cases, enlargement of the liver, coma, and even death can occur; in the Malay Archipelago and New Guinea, the documented mortality rate is over 25%. Children under the age of 12 are most vulnerable, and in one global assessment accounted for 68% of all fatalities. The toxin is not inactivated by cooking.

© Robert van Dam

Population Status: Classified as "critically endangered", the hawksbill is among the most endangered of all sea turtles. Global populations have been severely depleted due to over-harvest, and a significant part of this harvest has been for products made from their shell. In 1993 Japan (the world's largest importer of hawksbill shell) imposed a zero quota on the importation of hawksbill shell and shortly thereafter Cuba dramatically reduced its commercial harvest, a combination of factors that has contributed to rising numbers of hawksbills in the Caribbean Sea. Globally, however, the species is in crisis, with IUCN estimating a decline exceeding more than 80% in just three generations. A continuing problem for this species is the purchase of shell items, such as jewelry, by tourists (see pages 98, 99, and 110).

In the Caribbean, gravid (egg-bearing) female hawksbill sea turtles have been observed targeting the green calcareous seaweed *Halimeda*; it's thought that the female turtles may be doing this in order to obtain a source of calcium to incorporate into their eggshells. Gravid females in the Caribbean also eat coral rubble, presumably for the same reason.

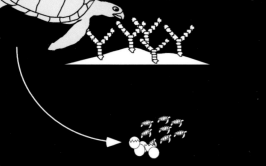

© Ursula Keuper-Bennett/Peter Bennett

Kemp's Ridley Sea Turtles (*Lepidochelys kempii*)

© Ursula Keuper-Bennett/Peter Bennett

Description: The rarest of all sea turtles, the Kemp's ridley averages 75 - 100 lbs. and 24-28 inches in shell length (with shell length and width being nearly equal). **Carapace** color is olive grey to grey, the plastron is yellowish; hatchlings, in contrast, are nearly black all over. There are five pairs of costal scutes and a single claw on each flipper. Maturity is reached at 10-15 years of age; comparatively young for a sea turtle.

Distribution: One of the most unique aspects of this species is that 95% of all nestings occur on a single beach at or near Rancho Nuevo, on the east coast of Mexico. The species is largely confined to the Gulf of Mexico, although individuals are sometimes encountered as far north as Maine and Nova Scotia and are occasionally found as far away as Morocco on the northwest coast of Africa. Adult habitat is characterized by muddy or sandy bottoms, where their primary prey, crustaceans and molluscs, are abundant.

Population Status: In 1947, more than 42,000 females were documented on film coming ashore to nest <u>on a single day</u>, but by 1978 there were fewer than 500 females nesting per *year*.

Since that time the population has begun to recover, due primarily to protection of nesting turtles and their nests in Mexico and required use of Turtle Exclusion Devices (TEDs) on shrimp trawlers in the Gulf of Mexico (see pages 67, 92).

Females typically lay three clutches of eggs per year, often nesting during daylight hours. Concern has been raised that the average number of eggs laid per **clutch** has decreased in recent years, but some experts view this as the result of more novice nesters … the natural result of an increasing population. Rising numbers of nesting Kemp's ridleys, including a small population beginning to establish itself on beaches in Texas, is a tribute to more than three decades of intensive bilateral conservation by the USA and Mexico. Continued emphasis on the use of TEDs in offshore waters is key to the survival of this ancient species.

CRITICALLY ENDANGERED **ENDANGERED**

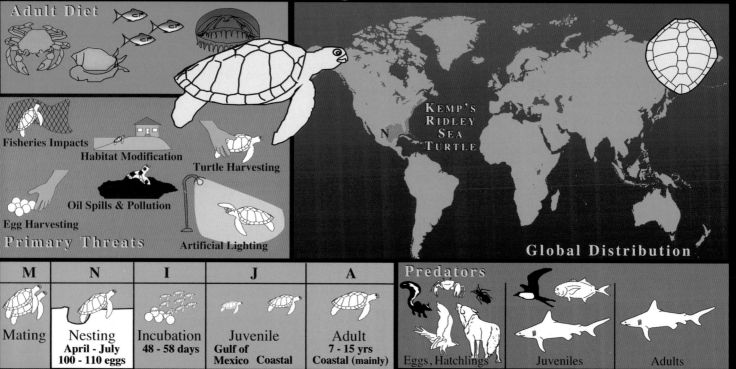

Adult Diet

Fisheries Impacts

Habitat Modification

Turtle Harvesting

Oil Spills & Pollution

Egg Harvesting

Primary Threats

Artificial Lighting

KEMP'S RIDLEY SEA TURTLE

Global Distribution

M	N	I	J	A
Mating	Nesting **April - July** **100 - 110 eggs**	Incubation **48 - 58 days**	Juvenile **Gulf of Mexico Coastal**	Adult **7 - 15 yrs** **Coastal (mainly)**

Predators

Eggs, Hatchlings | Juveniles | Adults

Olive Ridley Sea Turtles
(*Lepidochelys olivacea*)

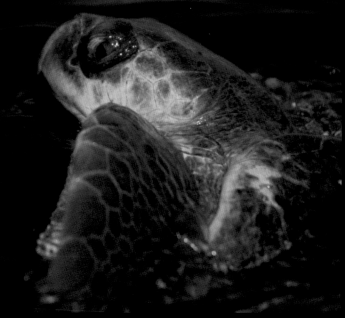

Description: The most numerous of sea turtles, the olive ridley is a small turtle with a disk-shaped **carapace**. Similar in size to Kemp's ridleys, adults average 75 - 100 lbs; shell length averages a mere 24-28 inches. Ridleys are unique in having inframarginal pores in the "bridge scutes" that connect carapace and plastron; the function of these pores is not fully known.

Distribution: Pan-tropical, it is found both in continental shelf habitats and in the open sea. Throughout their range olive ridleys often associate with floating objects, from driftwood to dead whales; given their wide dietary preferences the function of such behavior may be as much for prey capture as to avoid becoming a snack themselves.

Diet: Olive ridleys feed mainly on fish and invertebrates, including **salps**, molluscs, crustaceans (shrimp, crabs), sea urchins, barnacles and sea jellies. Foraging is often in soft bottom habitats, but off Baja California (Mexico) they appear to feed almost exclusively on pelagic red crabs which are superabundant in that area. An **omnivore** by nature, olive ridleys will take longline hooks baited with fish and squid. Off major nesting grounds in India, ridleys often become trapped in fishing trawls.

Nesting: Olive ridleys form nesting **arribadas** (see page 67), mostly along continental coasts, though often these nesting areas are separated from the mainland by lagoons or estuaries. Arribadas are synchronous mass nesting events where hundreds, sometimes hundreds of thousands, of egg-bearing females clamor onto the nesting beach at one time, and then repeat the spectacle on 28-day lunar associated cycles. Most females lay only two clutches of eggs during a reproductive season, depositing about 100 eggs per clutch ... and oftentimes dig up each other's nests in the drive to lay their own eggs. Olive ridleys are often seen in large groups traveling between breeding and feeding grounds.

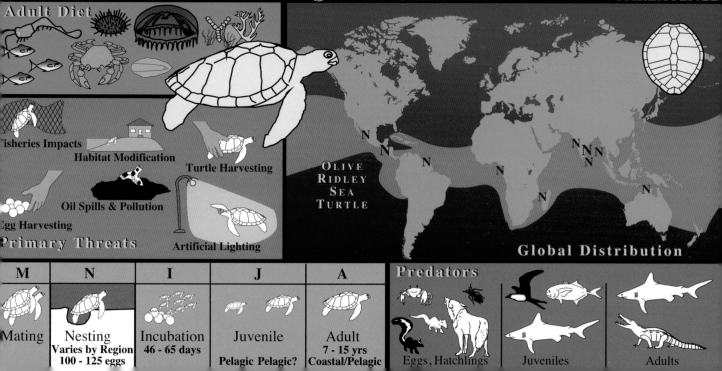

ENDANGERED   ENDANGERED THREATENED

Adult Diet

Fisheries Impacts
Habitat Modification
Turtle Harvesting
Oil Spills & Pollution
Egg Harvesting
Artificial Lighting

Primary Threats

OLIVE RIDLEY SEA TURTLE

Global Distribution

M	N	I	J	A
Mating	Nesting **Varies by Region** **100 - 125 eggs**	Incubation 46 - 65 days	Juvenile **Pelagic Pelagic?**	Adult **7 - 15 yrs** **Coastal/Pelagic**

Predators

| Eggs, Hatchlings | Juveniles | Adults |

Description: Originally listed as a member of the genus *Chelonia* (with the green sea turtle), the flatback was recently re-classified into its own genus, *Natator*. This relatively small sea turtle, typically 35 inches in carapace length as an adult, is restricted to the continental shelf of Australia (including southern Irian Jaya and the Gulf of Papua) where it tends to inhabit turbid bays and calm coastal areas.

The form of the body is flattened compared to other sea turtles, with an unkeeled carapace that is slightly serrated posteriorly. Carapace color is gray to pale green. Carapace scutes thin and considerably less keratinized than other sea turtles, making it difficult to see seams between the scutes in older adults.

Diet: Flatbacks are largely carnivorous, feeding primarily on jellyfish and soft-bodied invertebrates, including sea cucumbers, sea pens, and soft corals.

Nesting: The largest rookery is Crab Island in the Gulf of Carpentaria. Females nest nocturnally approximately every two weeks during the summer. Hatchlings emerge from their nests and scurry to the sea, as

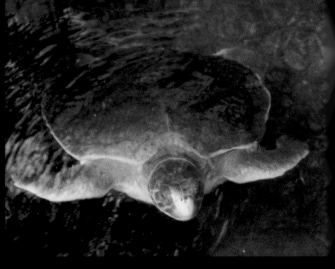

would any other sea turtle hatchling, but young juveniles are <u>not</u> thought to have a pelagic existence, remaining instead in the nearshore environment of the adult. Flatback hatchlings are larger than other members of this family; this trait may provide something of a size refuge against general predation in the nearshore environment at this stage.

Threats: Protected throughout its range by the Australian government, small numbers are allowed to be taken for aboriginal harvest. Concerns exist relating to flatbacks getting caught in prawn trawls, modification of coastal nesting habitats through coastal development and agricultural practices, and pollution of nearshore waters where the flatback forages and rests.

DATA DEFICIENT

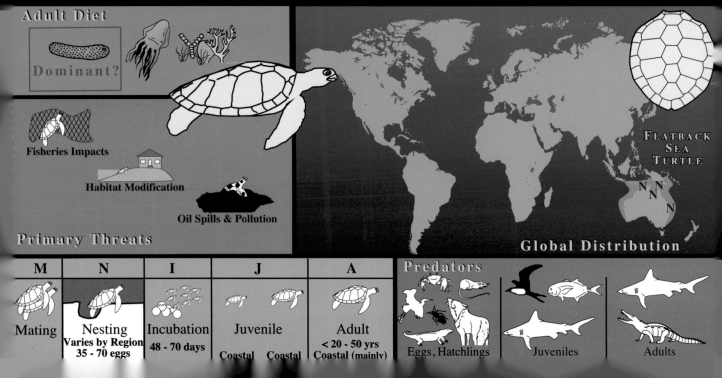

Adult Diet

Dominant?

Fisheries Impacts

Habitat Modification

Oil Spills & Pollution

Primary Threats

FLATBACK SEA TURTLE

N N N N

Global Distribution

Predators

M	N	I	J	A
Mating	Nesting **Varies by Region 35 - 70 eggs**	Incubation **48 - 70 days**	Juvenile Coastal Coastal	Adult **< 20 - 50 yrs** Coastal (mainly)

Eggs, Hatchlings   Juveniles   Adults

WHAT DO SEA TURTLES EAT?

A Short Guide to Dining Out with Sea Turtles

For the most part, a sea turtle's diet will vary as it matures. In general, as very young juveniles living amongst flotsam in open ocean **drift lines**, sea turtles feed on a variety of zooplankton, holoplankton, crustaceans and other invertebrates.

Lacking teeth, the jaws of sea turtles end in an easily recognized beak, which functions to bite, tear or crush prey items. As juveniles and adults, their primary diets are as follows.

GREEN SEA TURTLES
Green sea turtles have finely serrated beaks that allow them to crop a variety of seaweeds, from fine filamentous forms to large leafy types and seagrasses.

Many populations of green sea turtles throughout the world feed primarily on seagrasses, maintaining grazing plots where individuals selectively feed. By cropping the new growth within the plots, the turtles gain a food source of higher quality (young seagrasses often are higher in nitrogen and lower in lignin concentrations). Additionally, green sea turtles make use of specialized hindgut microbial fermentation to digest the plant material, resulting in high amounts of released energy in the plant cells.

HAWKSBILL SEA TURTLES
The hawksbill derives its name from the narrow, protruding beak which resembles its namesake. The unique shape allows this sea turtle to eat a variety of food items often lodged within cracks and crevices of the reef. Prey are most often sponges, but may also include invertebrates such as ascidians and molluscs, and even the occasional seagrass.

As a card-carrying spongivore, hawksbills are one of the few non-invertebrates adapted to feed on marine sponges as a major part of their diet. This allows them access to a unique food source that most other organisms cannot consume due to protective spicules (imagine little shards of glass) and toxins.

LEATHERBACK SEA TURTLES
The pointed cusps and sharp-edged jaws of the leatherback are perfectly designed for grabbing and ripping apart siphonophores, jellies, and their many cousins. Backward-pointing flexible spines in the leatherback's mouth and throat help swallow the chomped-up gelatinous tidbits and direct them "down" towards the turtle's stomach.

Jellyfish wouldn't seem to be the most nutritious diet in the world, but clearly they sustain these massive turtles, many of whom weigh more than a ton. The diet may also be supplemented by zooplankton, small fish and other critters trapped in the tentacles or stomachs of their prey.

OTHER SEA TURTLE SPECIES
Loggerhead – With jaws designed for crushing and grinding, this species feeds primarily on molluscs and crustaceans; there are also reports of this animal feeding on mangrove leaves, jellies, and fish … a true omnivore.

Olive Ridley - Found in a wide variety of coastal and oceanic habitats, olive ridleys prey on crustaceans, molluscs, gastropods, jellyfish and salps, fish and fish eggs, and even algae.

Kemp's Ridley – As in the case of the olive ridley, the juvenile diet is poorly known. However, as adults, this species has a strong preference for the taste of crab (almost any type of crab!).

Flatback – Feeds primarily on soft-bodied benthic invertebrates, including sea cucumbers, soft corals and sea pens.

Feeding Adaptations

Leatherback Sea Turtle

Green Sea Turtle

Piercing

Sharply pointed upper and lower jaw cusps allow this animal to pierce sea jellies and other soft-bodied animals in the open sea. Leatherbacks feed both at the surface, and at great depth. Backward pointing spines in the leatherback's pallet and esophagus help guide and move the soft food towards the stomach.

Scraping

Serrated upper jaw effectively scrapes filamentous algae off hard bottoms, and shears leafy seaweeds and seagrasses. Green turtles have an active gut flora to assist them in breaking down otherwise undigestible vegetative matter.

Hawksbill Sea Turtle

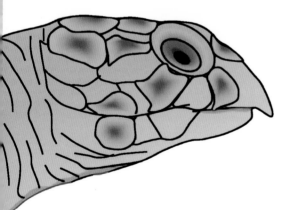

Loggerhead Sea Turtle

Cutting

The bird-like beak consisting of an overhanging upper jaw allows this animal to slice into and bite-off chunks of sponges attached to the bottom, and to feed on sponges and other invertebrates in the crevices of tropical and subtropical reefs and other hard-bottom habitats.

Crushing

Strong musculature and a wide upper and lower jaw allows loggerheads to grab molluscs and mobile crustaceans, such as horseshoe crabs. Bony plates inside the mouth allow crushing of the prey's hard shell. Imagine having a conch salad, shell and all!

Life as an Aquatic Herbivore
Anatomy of a Vegan Turtle's Meal

Did you know that over 275 different species of seaweed have been identified as being fed upon by green sea turtles in the Hawaiian Islands?!!

Plant material is pretty tough stuff to digest; the green sea turtle's digestive system is broken down into discrete sections, each with their own role to play.

The large intestine is where most of the microflora live that conduct microbial digestion of the plant cellulose. In green turtles, this is where most of the particle breakdown occurs.

The cloaca is where undigested material is discharged as fecal pellets

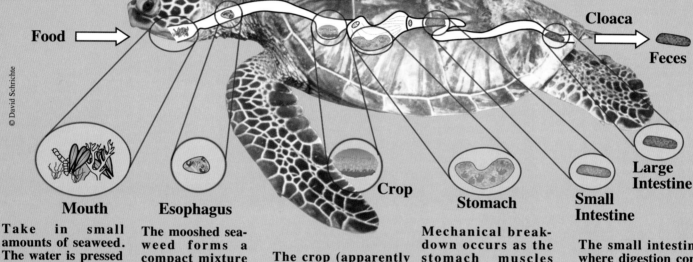

© David Schrichte

Food

Cloaca

Feces

Mouth

Esophagus

Crop

Stomach

Small Intestine

Large Intestine

Mouth
Take in small amounts of seaweed. The water is pressed out by pushing the food up against the roof of its mouth prior to swallowing.

Esophagus
The mooshed seaweed forms a compact mixture called a bolus as it travels through the esophagus.

The crop (apparently found only in Hawaiian green sea turtles) serves as a storage space prior to entry to the stomach.

Mechanical breakdown occurs as the stomach muscles churn the food. Cellular and chemical breakdown commence with the secretion of acids and enzymes.

The small intestine is where digestion continues and absorption begins. In carnivores this structure is short, while in herbivores such as green turtles it is long. In between the small and large intestine is a structure called a caecum which may serve to store the material and increase the digestion time.

© Ursula Keuper-Bennett/Peter Bennett

(Don't try this at home, professional scatologist)

Collection of green sea turtle feces by researchers can help solve the puzzle regarding what types of algae or seagrass a specific population is feeding on and provide clues related to an individual turtle's overall health.

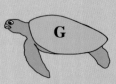

G

And it's not any easier for a tried & true jellivore...

Anatomy of a Jelly-Eating Leatherback

Sea jellies (jellyfish) are mostly water and it's likely that leatherbacks, which as adults often weigh more than 1,000 pounds, need to consume large numbers of them at a single feeding. By migrating into temperate and even subarctic waters where large jellies are more common, leatherbacks maximize their caloric intake!

Compared with really large jellies seen in temperate and colder waters, the jellies of the tropics make a wimpy meal...

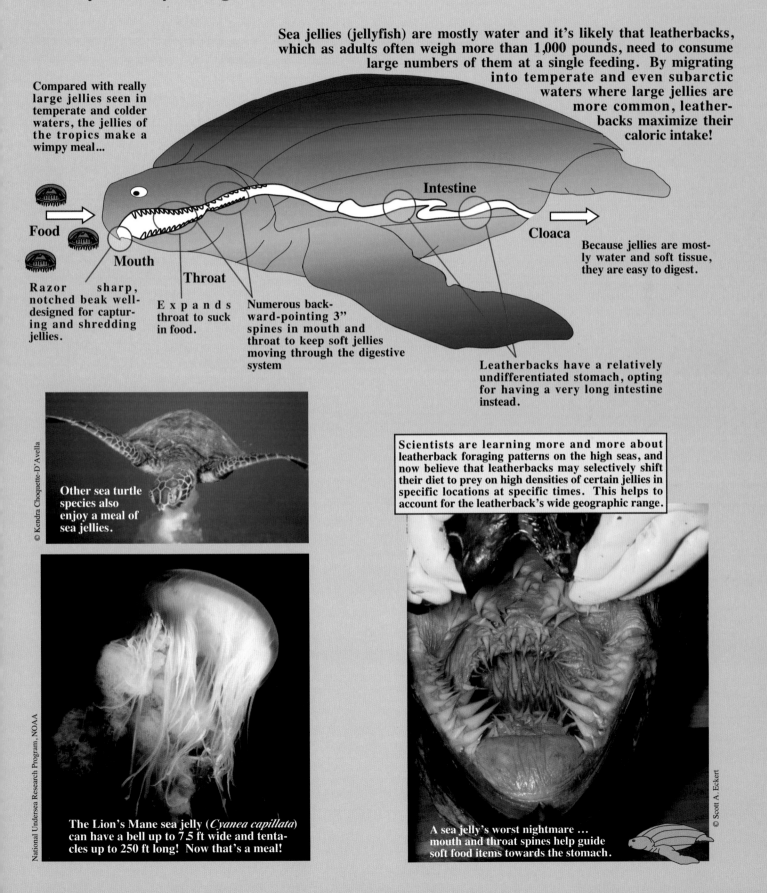

Food

Mouth

Razor sharp, notched beak well-designed for capturing and shredding jellies.

Throat

Expands throat to suck in food.

Numerous back-ward-pointing 3" spines in mouth and throat to keep soft jellies moving through the digestive system

Intestine

Cloaca

Because jellies are mostly water and soft tissue, they are easy to digest.

Leatherbacks have a relatively undifferentiated stomach, opting for having a very long intestine instead.

Other sea turtle species also enjoy a meal of sea jellies.

Scientists are learning more and more about leatherback foraging patterns on the high seas, and now believe that leatherbacks may selectively shift their diet to prey on high densities of certain jellies in specific locations at specific times. This helps to account for the leatherback's wide geographic range.

© Kendra Choquette-D'Avella

National Undersea Research Program, NOAA

The Lion's Mane sea jelly (*Cyanea capillata*) can have a bell up to 7.5 ft wide and tentacles up to 250 ft long! Now that's a meal!

A sea jelly's worst nightmare ... mouth and throat spines help guide soft food items towards the stomach.

© Scott A. Eckert

Sea Turtles as Keystone Species

What is a Keystone Species?

Often in nature, a specific predator within an ecosystem will play a major role in determining the community structure. Such keystone species can be either carnivores or herbivores, and frequently function to prevent resource monopolization by a prey species within a community. Removal of such organisms causes dramatic changes and sometimes these changes will cascade through the ecosystem.

(A) The Role of Green Sea Turtles in Seagrass Productivity & Abundance

Green sea turtles can function as keystone species in that their actions in certain seagrass environments can alter the community structure and dynamics of these habitats. Through their selective grazing activities (cropping of seagrasses) in the Caribbean Sea, for example, characteristic "grazing plots" are sometimes formed. Here the turtle functions as a natural disturbance, similar to storm waves, creating a situation which not only promotes growth, but prevents competitive exclusion by certain faster-growing seagrass species. Biochemically, younger seagrass blades are easier to digest, and higher in nutritional nitrogen (required for protein synthesis in herbivores), while older blades often contain more hard-to-digest structural materials. Through selective grazing, the sea turtles maintain grazing plots full of young blades that invest more of their available energy in nitrogen and starch than in structural components, which benefits not only the sea turtles, but also a wide host of other macro- and microherbivores. As such, green sea turtles can determine whether a seagrass habitat is herbivore- or detritivore-dominated.

Green sea turtles can modify a seagrass community in terms of the primary productivity, plant recovery and detrital production

Lack of Cropping

Cropping

Ungrazed blades lead to fewer and larger plants, which results in overall less biomass of seagrass than in smaller, more plentiful leaves. Old, decrepit plants slowly breakdown in a detrital environment.

"Grazing Plot"
Fresh young leaves with higher nutritional content; more leaves and higher biomass.

Over time, grazed plots contribute importantly to coastal processes (stabilizing sediments, recycling nutrients) and offer food and shelter to a healthy array of smaller herbivores.

Detritivore-Dominated Seagrass Community

Herbivore-Dominated Seagrass Community

Loss of Ecological Function

In areas where green sea turtle populations are decreased, seagrass growth would not be controlled by cropping, resulting in older and larger seagrass blades and, over time, relatively larger amounts of detritus. In such a community, detritivores would be expected to dominate.

Florida Keys National Marine Sanctuary, NOAA

Florida Keys National Marine Sanctuary, NOAA

Ⓑ How Hawksbills Help Maintain Biodiversity Through a Diet of Glass!!!

Hawksbill sea turtles can function as keystone species on certain coral reefs where sponges predominate. Studies of Caribbean hawksbills show that the species feeds selectively on only a few groups ("Orders") of sponges: namely, Astrophorida, Hadromerida, and Spirophorida. This high selectivity may result in rarer species becoming established and competing successfully for space and nutrients on the reef.

Ⓒ   The Paradox of Leatherbacks as Bycatch

For years, commercial fishers have noted a dramatic increase in the jellyfish populations occurring in the Atlantic Ocean; often these jellies will concentrate in specific regions of the open ocean where they feed on the larval forms of commercially-important food fish. The concern is that large numbers of jellyfish will result in fewer fish larvae surviving, resulting in fewer large fish for the fishermen to catch. One of the primary predators on these jellyfish populations is the leatherback sea turtle. Ironically, the primary cause of mortality for the leatherback sea turtle is accidental capture (or bycatch, see page 88) by commercial fishers. Because leatherbacks may play such a dominant role in controlling the large jelly populations in the Atlantic Ocean, the continued demise of this species through commercial fishing activities may doom both the industry and the turtles.

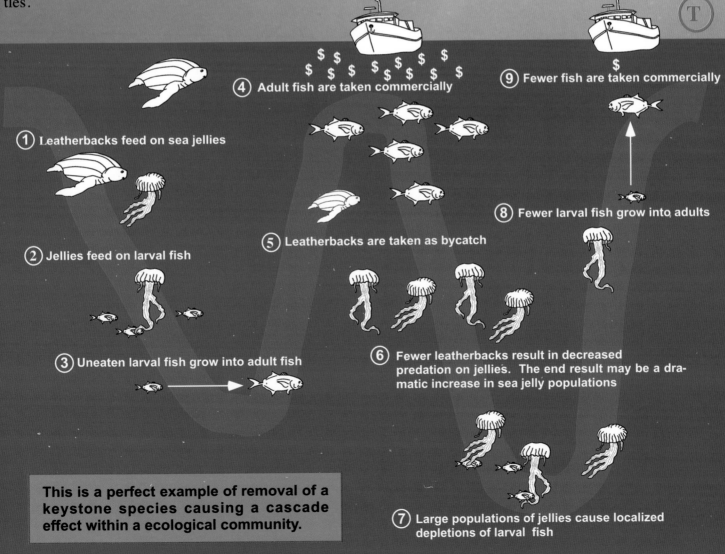

④ Adult fish are taken commercially

⑨ Fewer fish are taken commercially

① Leatherbacks feed on sea jellies

⑧ Fewer larval fish grow into adults

② Jellies feed on larval fish

⑤ Leatherbacks are taken as bycatch

③ Uneaten larval fish grow into adult fish

⑥ Fewer leatherbacks result in decreased predation on jellies. The end result may be a dramatic increase in sea jelly populations

This is a perfect example of removal of a keystone species causing a cascade effect within a ecological community.

⑦ Large populations of jellies cause localized depletions of larval fish

Resource Allocation

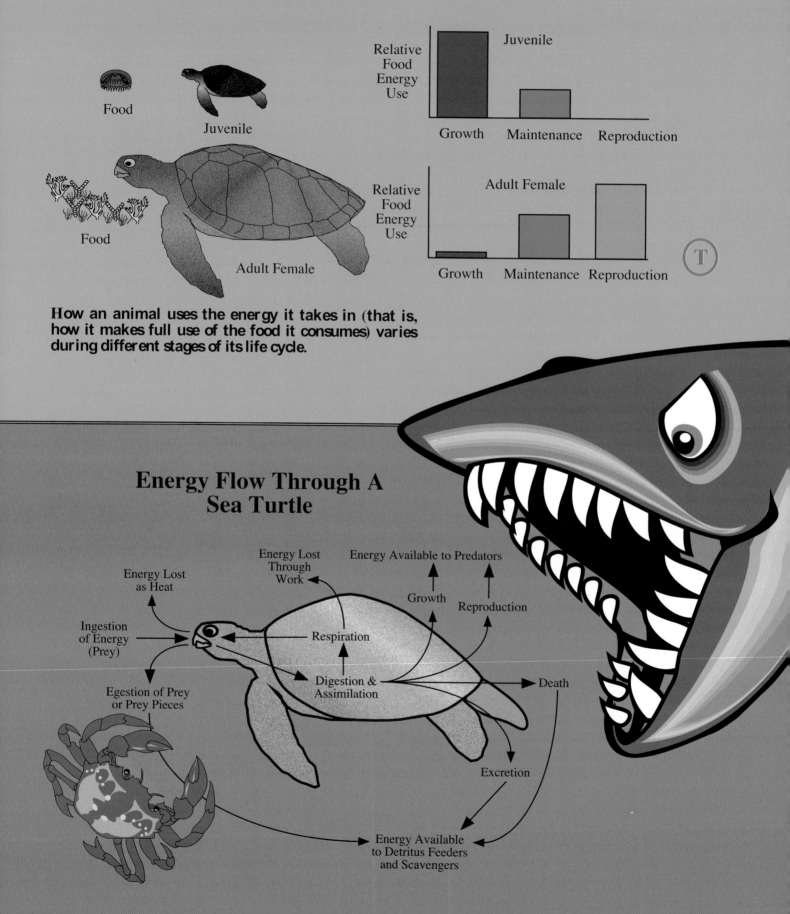

Juvenile

Relative Food Energy Use

Growth | Maintenance | Reproduction

Adult Female

Relative Food Energy Use

Growth | Maintenance | Reproduction

Food

Juvenile

Food

Adult Female

How an animal uses the energy it takes in (that is, how it makes full use of the food it consumes) varies during different stages of its life cycle.

Energy Flow Through A Sea Turtle

Energy Lost as Heat

Energy Lost Through Work

Energy Available to Predators

Growth

Reproduction

Ingestion of Energy (Prey)

Respiration

Egestion of Prey or Prey Pieces

Digestion & Assimilation

Death

Excretion

Energy Available to Detritus Feeders and Scavengers

PREDATORS ON SEA TURTLES

Eggs & Hatchlings   **Hatchlings & Juveniles**   **Subadults & Adults**

The highest predation rates for sea turtles (like most marine organisms) occur during the egg, **hatchling** and young **juvenile** stages. In addition to the ants, crabs, raccoons, foxes, coyotes, vultures and other scavenging **predators** that might dig into a nest to eat eggs, bacterial conditions in the nest can also destroy many eggs before they hatch. Many of the same beasties that would dig into a nest for the eggs will also prey on the emerging hatchlings; they in turn are joined by a variety of chasers and grabbers, including seabirds and a suite of reef and **pelagic** fish to which a hatchling or young juvenile would make quite a tasty meal. As sea turtles grow they gain defense against natural predators through the hardening and thickening of their shells.

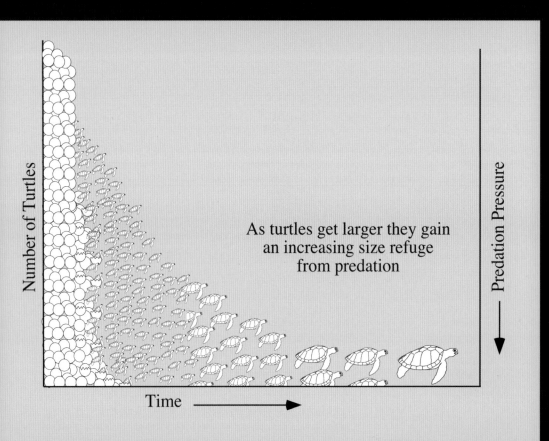

As turtles get larger they gain an increasing size refuge from predation

Additionally a refuge of sorts is created by virtue of their large size relative to many predators. As adults, sea turtles have very few natural predators other than orca ("killer") whales and a variety of sharks.

Crabs

© Scott A. Eckert

A wide range of crustacean species may feed upon eggs and hatchlings, from beach-dwelling crabs such as ghost crabs (*Ocypode* spp.), to reef species such as portunid crabs.

Some crabs are well-adapted for sniffing (er, actually tasting) the location of buried eggs based upon secretions and decomposition of nest materials (see page 82). Many species can easily handle burrowing into shallow nests, and large crabs use their claws to snatch small hatchlings as they move across the beach.

Crabs are one of the few natural coastal predators that are active at night and therefore pose a risk to hatchlings trying to reach the ocean after leaving the nest. Crabs also burrow into incubating nests, ruining their chances of hatching successfully.

From another perspective, crabs excel at being scavengers and they help keep the beach clean by eating nest debris after the hatchlings are gone.

Seabirds

Primarily a daytime **predator**, seabirds hunt from above; as such, it can be extremely difficult for their marine prey to detect them early enough to take defensive action. For hatchling sea turtles, this problem is amplified by the need to go from the relative safety of their underground nest across open territory (the beach) and into the water where they must frequently surface to breathe. **Hatchlings** deal with the first problem by often emerging in the evening or at night when seabirds are less active. Despite this behavioral strategy, paté of hatchling is a common component of many a seabird's guts and confirms that predation is occurring. Once the sea turtles reach a certain size, they gain a size refuge from such predation pressure; and, in fact, they may serve as a host for seabirds at sea (see page 55)!

Most seabirds are well-adapted for detecting and capturing small prey. Their well-developed eyes detect prey from the air and a quick, short dive into the water results in a hatchling being grabbed for consumption. Other birds, such as night herons, wait for the dinner bell; they pace back and forth along the beach and actually listen for sounds of hatchlings digging up through the sand!

The amount of predation by seabirds varies with the species involved and the geographic location. To reduce their vulnerability, some sea turtle species have specific anti-predator defenses while in their hatchling stage. For example, hatchling coloration (see page 73), specifically dark coloration on the dorsal (or top) side may reflect an adaptation for minimizing detection from above when the hatchlings are in the ocean. A seabird looking down sees only the dark surface waters. A pale-colored hatchling, on the other hand, would be easy prey.

A "hatchling-eye-view" of a predator. Frigate birds like this are a hatchlings' worst nightmare in many parts of the tropical Pacific.

© Kendra Choquette-D'Avella

© Robert I. Pitman

Fish

Sea turtles lay an unusually large number of eggs for a reptile, effectively balancing high rates of mortality during the early portions of a turtle's life. In an intriguing Australian study that involved attaching hatchling green sea turtles to fishing lines and measuring the amount of line deployed as the hatchling made its way across the beach and reef towards the open ocean prior to it being snatched-up by a predator, scientists were able to quantify where predation risk was greatest against hatchlings prior to entering the "lost year" phase of their life history. The data showed the strongest predation pressure occurred whilst crossing the reef itself, usually within the first hour after entering the sea; during this period up to 97% of the hatchlings were eaten prior to clearing the reef. The characteristic "swim frenzy" observed in hatchlings immediately after entering the water may be an evolutionary response designed to decrease exposure to nearshore predatory fishes.

The Usual Suspects

Groupers
Large predators that have territories atop reefs and on the reef slope. Groupers excel at short lunges and ambushing their prey.

Jacks
Roaming predators that can chase down their prey, some jacks hunt in packs. This group of fish ranges from deeper offshore waters all they way into the shallower reef flats.

Snappers
Fast-moving, schooling predators. Most species are deeper water, but some are extremely active near reef slopes.

Eels
Reef flat and reef slope predators that can be effective night-time hunters. Eels often roam nearshore and shallow reef waters searching for their prey using a variety of senses, including taste.

© David Schrichte

Sharks

The tooth of a tiger shark is perfectly designed for slicing into, and through, the hard carapace of a sea turtle.

Sharks are among the only predators capable of preying on all life stages of sea turtles. Large sharks such as tiger sharks are well-adapted for feeding on both sub-adult and adult turtles. Sharks can actively feed both during the day and at night. They hunt using of an array of senses, ranging from long-distance taste to close-distance detection of electrical impulses from their prey. In nearshore waters, the use of vision (in terms of detecting basic "turtle-like" shapes floating on the surface) by the hunting shark might account for a variety of shark attacks on humans boogey-boarding, surfing, snorkeling or swimming. Tiger sharks captured in the Caribbean Sea sometimes contain remains from several hawksbill sea turtles.

THE BIOLOGICAL ARMS RACE

As one country acquires a new form of weapon to threaten another, this in turn encourages the threatened country to spend large amounts of money developing or otherwise acquiring a more powerful counter-weapon. The first country then has to make its weapons more powerful to counteract the threat, and so on… The result has been dubbed an "arms race".

In nature, co-evolution between predators and prey often leads to a form of "biological arms race", with each side evolving new adaptations over generations in response to "escalations" (recent adaptations) by the other. You can imagine that shark predation, for example, may select against slower-moving or thinner-shelled sea turtles; leaving primarily faster-moving or thicker-shelled sea turtles to successfully reproduce and pass on the genes for these traits. Similarly, this may lead, over time, to selection against slow-moving, ineffectively-toothed sharks, which starve when they cannot get enough food.

A number of behaviors, such as basking (pages 56 - 57), mating in shallow water (page 59), and resting in holes on the reef, may be, in part, a reaction to predation pressure by large sharks. As with seabirds, the amount of predation by sharks varies with the species involved, prey preferences, and the ecological conditions between geographic locations. Juvenile, sub-adult and adult coloration, both dorsally (top) and ventrally (bottom), may reflect an adaptation for minimizing detection. Detection occurs when sharks look down into the water column for turtles feeding or resting, or when sharks gaze up toward the surface. Many young turtles have darker dorsal coloration (to blend into the deeper waters or bottom habitat) and lighter ventral coloration (to blend into the surface waters when viewed from below); this type of coloration is seen in a wide variety of swimming animals and is called counter-shading.

THE VIEW FROM BELOW:

On occasion sharks may mistake the wayward paddleboarder and other recreational aquatic forms for sea turtles.

Tasty turtle morsel or the human-equivalent of brussel sprouts???

Predation Avoidance Strategies

Sea turtles are often characterized as slow-moving animals that protect themselves with armored coverings. While this may be one example of a defensive strategy, sea turtles actually possess a wide range of strategies, some of which are used at different stages of their life histories.

Crypsis
Coloration often provides a certain level of protection by helping sea turtles blend into their surroundings.

Escape Behavior
Most sea turtles can produce short bursts of speed from their powerful foreflippers.

Structural Deterrents
The hard shell (carapace) covers the vulnerable internal organs essential for life functions (heart, lungs, liver... you know - all the gushy ones).

Chemical Deterrents
Hawksbill sea turtles may gain some protection from incorporating toxic compounds found in prey organisms associated with tropical coral reefs.

Behavioral Deterrents
Sleeping in holes: greens and hawksbills are known to sleep wedged in holes and over-hangs amongst the coral reefs. Such behavior serves to protect the exposed head and limbs of the animal from predation.

Some turtles may turn sideways, presenting a bony shield to potential predators; others may dive deeply, below the capabilities of the predators chasing them, or become aggressive and attempt to bite potential predators.

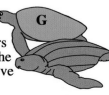

SEA TURTLES AND SYMBIOSIS

Symbiosis is a relationship between two different organisms

Types of Sea Turtle Symbiosis

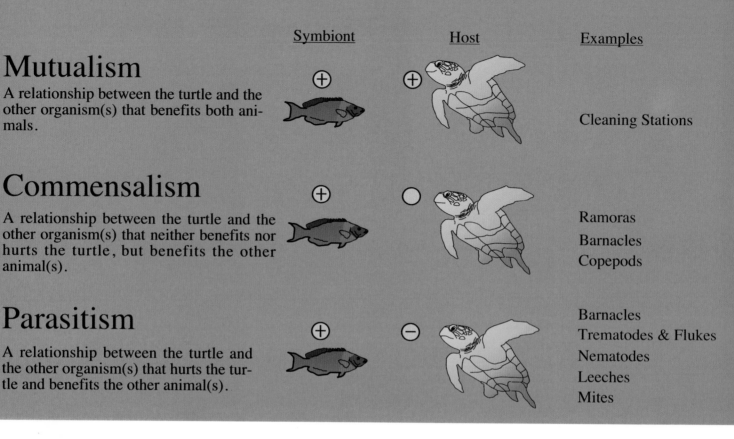

	Symbiont	Host	Examples

Mutualism

A relationship between the turtle and the other organism(s) that benefits both animals.

Cleaning Stations

Commensalism

A relationship between the turtle and the other organism(s) that neither benefits nor hurts the turtle, but benefits the other animal(s).

Ramoras
Barnacles
Copepods

Parasitism

A relationship between the turtle and the other organism(s) that hurts the turtle and benefits the other animal(s).

Barnacles
Trematodes & Flukes
Nematodes
Leeches
Mites

© Scott A. Eckert

A number of sea turtle species (loggerheads in particular) often carry huge numbers of **epibionts**. Probably the most well known are the barnacles, most of which filter feed and use the turtle's shell as an attachment point from which they can sample the ocean's currents for delectable planktonic treats. One particular barnacle, *Chelonibia caretta*, is known to grow "roots" through the turtle's scutes and into its bones, forming a very firm anchor against dislodgement. When barnacles do settle upon a host turtle, they tend to congregate in small groups. In part, this is done to facilitate reproduction as barnacles are hermaphroditic and are capable of cross-fertilizing adjacent barnacles through use of one of the longest penises (relative to body size) in the animal kingdom. Most barnacles are commensals, but some, like *Stephanolepas muricata,* are parasitic, burrowing into the skin and preying upon the internal tissues of their turtle hosts.

Like all organisms, sea turtles are susceptible to disease. Among the vectors suspected to be involved and found associated with sea turtles include viruses, bacteria, fungi, protozoans (Sargomastigophora and Apicomplexa), trematode flatworms, cestode flatworms, nematode worms, leeches, mites, and crustaceans. Parasites include flukes in both the heart and major arteries; other species of flukes have also been found in the gastrointestinal tract of certain turtles.

Commensal Barnacle
Note feeding activity.

© Ursula Keuper-Bennett/Peter Bennett

Parasitic Barnacles
on Lower Neck

Being an obligate herbivore comes with its own set of problems. Plant material is high in cellulose, a material that is extremely difficult for the average vertebrate to digest. Green sea turtles get around this by maintaining specialized microorganisms in their gut that assist in preparing plant material for digestion. In order to maintain this cellulytic bacterial stew, turtles need to slow the passage of plant material to give the bacteria enough time to digest their meal, while at the same time providing a suitable environment for them to flourish. So how do you pick up these wonderful little beasties if you've spent your earliest years living as a carnivore, a young juvenile in the open ocean? When juveniles recruit into grazing areas where subadult and adults have already been feeding, it may be that by ingesting the feces of their elders (the non-gross term for this is tactfully called **scatophagy**), they can innoculate themselves with the proper microflora.

Cleaning Station

© Ursula Keuper-Bennett/Peter Bennett

Ⓣ

Cleaning behavior is seen with sea turtles all over the world. In most cases this involves herbivorous fish, such as surgeonfish, that feed on seaweeds found growing atop the turtle's shell. Such behavior is advantageous for the turtle as it removes a major source of drag (see page 22), resulting in less energy usage, faster escape speeds, and easier movement through the fluid environment.

In the Hawaiian Islands, a few sites have been found where carnivorous fish, such as the endemic Saddleback Wrasse (*Thallasoma duperrey*), clean green sea turtles. These fish are thought to remove parasitic and commensal barnacles attached to the turtle's skin and shell. By taking advantage of an unusual food source (compared to the dietary habits of most reef fish), a unique ecological **niche** is created!

Herbivorous Cleaning

© Ursula Keuper-Bennett/Peter Bennett

Carnivorous cleaning may play a role in the spread of a tumorous disease (see pages 79 - 80) from turtle to turtle. As the fish remove small parasites, commensals, and bits of tissue, they may be taking up diseased tissue and passing the disease itself onto the next turtle(s) that they "clean". Working out such relationships involves extensive detective work by a variety of turtle and fish ecologists, veterinarians and disease specialists.

© Kendra Choquette-D'Avella

Carnivorous Cleaning

© Ursula Keuper-Bennett/Peter Bennett

Ⓖ

Remora are a very specialized commensal fish adapted to hitchhike with large turtles, gaining both protection and a free ride.

In some areas of the South Pacific, fishermen tie a rope to a remora and then throw it back into the ocean. The remora seeks out the largest animal nearby to attach itself to and seek refuge, sometimes this is a sea turtle. As the fisherman applies pressure to the rope, the remora holds onto the turtle with its suction disc even tighter. Eventually the fisherman hauls the turtle aboard his boat. The end result is that the remora acts as a "living fishing hook" which hones in on the fisherman's prey on its own!

As shown on the next page, it's not unusual for turtles at sea to function as Fish Aggregation Devices (FADs) for a variety of juvenile fish seeking shelter from predators in open water. Interestingly, there are a number of species of fish that specialize, as adults, in associating with large marine animals. Pilotfish, *Nucrates ductor*, are often found swimming underneath oceanic sharks, marine mammals, and sea turtles. While such a close association benefits the pilotfish by providing protection and a form of transport (pilotfish are thought to "ride" the boundary layer associated with their host, much like a dolphin rides the bow-wave in front of a ship), the fish might also be providing their hosts with a service by "cleaning" external parasites. The fish may also enjoy the table scraps left over by the fine dining habits of their hosts. The suckerfishes, or remoras, have taken this strategy one step further. These animals have a highly modified dorsal fin which functions as a suction cup and serves to attach them for periods of time to their hosts.

Sea Turtles as FADs and as Aircraft Carriers

At sea, it's not unusual to find seabirds perched atop floating, resting sea turtles. Such a relationship may assist sea turtles through a subtle form of cleaning behavior whereby the birds preferentially pick-off hitchhikers that would otherwise increase drag to the turtle when moving through the water. On the other hand, the turtle provides an important resting perch for many seabirds at sea.

Occasionally, the seabirds resting atop the turtle's back will grab a snack from the fish resting beneath it.

Given their habit of floating mostly motionless for long periods of time on the surface, sea turtles can function as Fish Aggregating Devices (FADs) in the open ocean.

Advantages
By sheltering underneath sea turtles, small fish gain the protection of the turtle's large size.

Disadvantages
Aggregations of species tend to attract the interests of predators that would not normally bother sea turtles. On a number of occasions sea turtles have been found impaled by the spikes of marlins or swordfish. Presumably, they were accidentally impaled as these predators attempted to get at the fish sheltering beneath the turtle.

© Robert L. Pitman

BASKING BEHAVIOR

Basking behavior, where turtles lie motionless and soak-up the heat of the sun, is common in freshwater turtles and tortoises. Basking is also seen in marine turtles, but it appears to be confined to the Galapagos Islands and the Northwestern Hawaiian Islands (NWHI) and its function may be more complex. And while there is no denying that basking behavior allows the animal to absorb large amounts of solar radiation, sea turtles do not tend to change their position relative to the position of the sun. In fact, increased body temperature from solar radiation may limit the time the animal can spend basking.

Black rock crabs *(Grapsus sp.)* have been observed feeding on algae atop basking sea turtles, in essence a form of terrestrial cleaning behavior.

In the NWHI, both male and female green sea turtles have been observed lying motionless on isolated beaches, even at night. Daytime basking behavior probably plays a significant role in thermoregulation; solar raising of internal body temperature would increase rates of metabolism, which in turn could lead to faster digestion and possibly increasing the rate of egg maturation in the female. However, such behavior occurring at night calls for other rationales. The reefs of the NWHI are dominated by large apex predators (such as sharks), a situation rare today on most other large-scale coral reef ecosystems. Additionally, captive studies in Hawai'i have shown that metabolic rates drop during basking behavior, suggesting that perhaps this nocturnal behavior in parts of Hawai'i may function to both decrease predation pressure from tiger sharks and to conserve energy.

Sometimes sea turtles are seen floating on the surface, far out to sea, for long periods of time during the day. This aquatic behavior is often termed "surface basking" and its advantages include conserving energy, avoiding predators, and raising body temperature. Studies have shown that green turtles raise their body temperatures by up to 5° C while surface basking. Smaller turtles such as the olive ridley are often seen associated with floating rafts of seaweed; whether this is also a form of basking or a way to increase prey capture (or avoid capture themselves) is still unanswered.

© David Schrichte

Heat Exchange and Other Functions of Basking

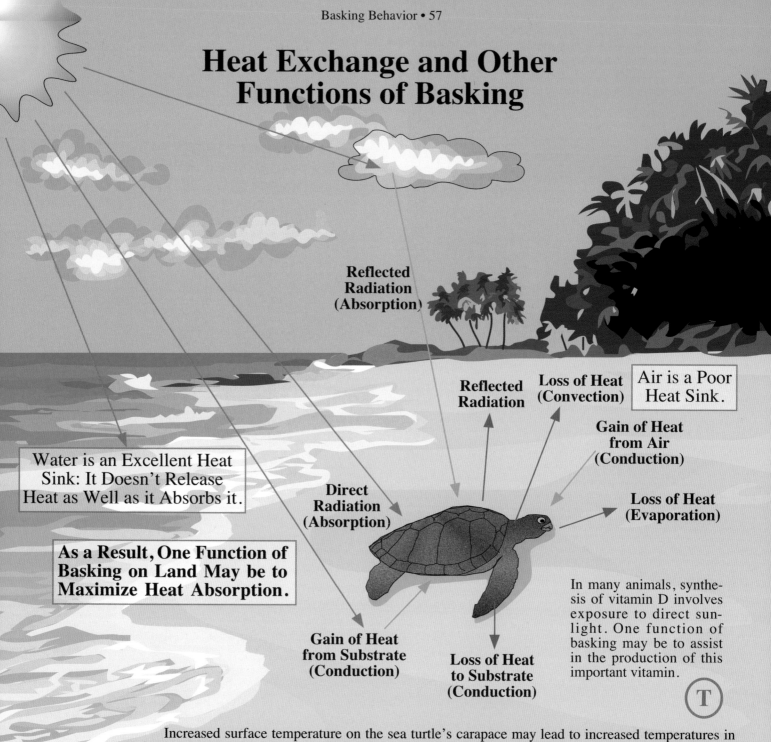

Reflected Radiation (Absorption)

Reflected Radiation

Loss of Heat (Convection)

Air is a Poor Heat Sink.

Gain of Heat from Air (Conduction)

Water is an Excellent Heat Sink: It Doesn't Release Heat as Well as it Absorbs it.

Direct Radiation (Absorption)

Loss of Heat (Evaporation)

As a Result, One Function of Basking on Land May be to Maximize Heat Absorption.

In many animals, synthesis of vitamin D involves exposure to direct sunlight. One function of basking may be to assist in the production of this important vitamin.

Gain of Heat from Substrate (Conduction)

Loss of Heat to Substrate (Conduction)

Increased surface temperature on the sea turtle's carapace may lead to increased temperatures in the lungs which lie directly underneath it (see page 18). Through the lungs, heat can be transferred into the circulatory system, which can efficiently distribute it throughout the body. Another possibility is that high carapace temperatures will translate into higher temperatures in the subdermal fatty tissues directly beneath it. This might have two results, the first of which is that the fat will insulate the rest of the body from rapid heat increases that could be problematic; the second of which is potentially an increased mobilization of fat for metabolic use. For females, mobilization of fat reserves could serve as an important energy source during reproductive seasons.

In the NWHI, where subadult green sea turtles spend an average of 10% of the day basking, turtles haul out in areas exposed to trade winds and occasionally will be seen flipping sand onto their carapaces with their front flippers. Presumably, this behavior is in response to heat stress in the animal; sand atop the carapace may reflect away more solar radiation and assist in convecting heat away from the body.

The very act of basking would serve to eliminate natural predation risk on the animal from sharks for the period that the turtle is out of the water. Basking also prevents males from mating with unreceptive females, and may dry out and kill epiphytic algae growing atop the carapace. Other possible functions of basking may include increasing the rate of digestion or serving as an alternative to more traditional underwater reef resting sites, such as caves, reef holes and ledges.

MATING BEHAVIOR

> *The turtle lives 'twixt plated decks*
> *Which practically conceal its sex*
> *I think it clever of the turtle*
> *In such a fix to be so fertile*
> Ogden Nash (1890 – 1950)

Regardless of species, most nesting areas are located in the tropics and subtropics. Almost all species migrate between prime feeding areas and preferred nesting beaches. It's not unusual for these migrations to be hundreds if not thousands of miles long, representing a considerable energy investment on the part of the animals involved. The world record-holder for distance is the leatherback, which has been documented to travel 15,000 km (nearly 10,000 miles) in a single year.

Amazingly, many lines of evidence suggest that sea turtles return to the general location of their birth in order to nest; only the female comes ashore for the purpose of nesting.

Everything You Always Wanted to Know About Sexing Sea Turtles*

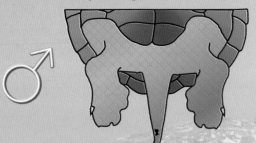 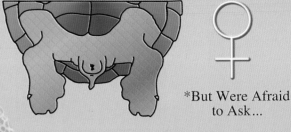

*But Were Afraid to Ask...

SEXUAL DIMORPHISM

As adults, males and females can be distinguished by the difference in tail length; adult males have characteristically long tails, curved claws on the flippers, and often a slightly concave (in-turned) plastron. All of these features assist the male during mating.

Immature turtles can not be sexed based on external characteristics. Scientists can determine sex by using laparoscopic examination, or by evaluating serum testosterone levels in the blood; such samples are often obtained from the sinus located in the turtle's neck. The sex of a turtle is easier to see in the case of adults. Mature males have a long, prehensile tail often extending noticeably beyond the rear edge of the carapace. There can also be dimorphism in the plastron in breeding age adults, with males showing a softer and slightly more concave shape to the plastron that may assist in securing his mount on the female.

© Robert Thorn

may nip the female's neck and flippers during mating and his claws may tear into her shell. The resulting wounds take weeks to properly heal and their presence can be used by scientists to determine which females have been successfully mated and are, therefore, most likely to nest that year. Because males will often try to dislodge other mating males (see box below), it's not only the female who may bear wounds from a mating incident. In captivity, pairs have been observed coupled together for periods of 10 hours or more. As things start to progress, the male will curl his long prehensile tail beneath the female in order to make contact with her cloaca. At this point the male's penis will erect into the female's cloaca and allow for the direct transfer of semen into both of the female's oviducts. The act of copulation may take several hours.

Sea turtles have internal fertilization, a relative rarity amongst the vast majority of marine animals. Most adult females do not mate every year (the Kemp's ridley is an exception), males are more likely to do so. This can result in very different reproductive patterns between adult males and females within a population, and annual reproductive activity may be different between the sexes for individuals of the same year class.

Courtship and mating in sea turtles occur weeks prior to nesting, and most studies show that successful mating tends to cease once nesting has commenced. Females store sperm from their pre-season couplings and use the stored sperm to fertilize several clutches throughout the nesting season.

Sea turtles are promiscuous breeders; long copulation periods and multiple partners help ensure viability for the many hundreds of eggs to be laid that year. Recent studies have shown that multiple paternity in the offspring during a single breeding season may vary according to species but is surprisingly rare, suggesting either sperm competition or first male preference through selective sperm storage by the female.

Mating is most often observed near the surface, but can occur anywhere in the water column. The male mounts the female from behind, no easy feat at sea! He holds on to the female's shell, in part by using enlarged claws on the foreflippers. Often a male

During mating season, males have been observed trying to mate with a wide variety of objects (including skin divers) which may, or may not, resemble a female sea turtle. In some places, fishermen make use of decoys, wooden objects (usually disk-shaped) that to an eager male turtle represent a potential mate. Once the male is focused on "mating" with the decoy, the fisherman can more easily capture him.

Females that are not "in the mood" have a number of options to employ to dissuade amorous males. One alternative is to retreat to an area away from where the males are congregated. Another possibility is to come ashore to bask; being "high and dry", while a very rare behavior among sea turtles, is clearly the ultimate in sea turtle frigidity. More common is for a female to fold her hind flippers together, in effect making it difficult for the male to mount her; a similar effect is achieved by a female positioning herself vertically in the water column facing an over-eager suitor.

Why Should Non-Mated Males Be Aggressive?

Possible outcomes involved in dislodging a mated male:

	Aggressive Mated Male	Non-aggressive Mated Male
Aggressive Male	⊕ May dislodge male during mating. ⊖ Potential high cost to conflict	⊕ Dislodges male during mating ⊖ Low cost to conflict
Non-aggressive Male	⊖ No dislodging = no mating No conflict = no cost	⊖ No dislodging = no mating No conflict = no cost

Thus, dislodging behavior by aggressive males is an evolutionary advantageous strategy as long as the gain (mating with the female turtle) is greater than the cost (loss of energy and and possible injury).

NESTING BEHAVIOR

So You Want To Be A Sea Turtle Do You????

Directions for Laying a Nest

1. Emerge from surf, be wary.
2. Those of you that might be ridleys need to emerge as a group and be able to pronounce 'arribada' correctly.
3. Direct ascent up the beach, try to look like you know what you're doing.
4. Select nest site. Temperature, high water markings, moisture, sand grain size, dune patterns and vegetation may all play a role.
5. Actively clear nest site of dry surface sand, debris and creeping vegetation.
6. Create "body pit"; if you're a green turtle, dig a proportional pit.
7. Excavate nest hole by alternating use of hind flippers.
8. Deposit eggs.
9. Carefully fill and pack nest chamber using hind flippers.
10. Disquise nest site, scuffle about, use front flippers to throw sand in all directions (extra points for burying researcher's expensive equipment).
11. Head back down the beach slope towards the sea.
12. Pause at ocean's edge and then re-enter the sea.

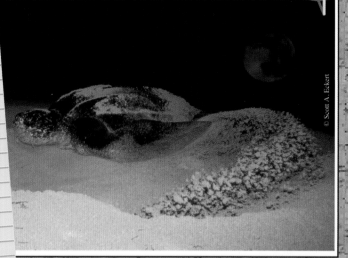

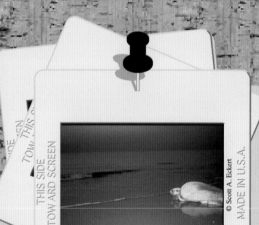

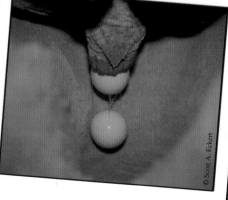

My vacation last year

Turtle Tracks: Identifying Turtle Species by the Footprints, er, Flipperprints They Leave Behind

Even hatchlings leave tracks...

As a turtle comes ashore, its flippers change from being used to swim and steer, to pulling (and pushing) its heavy body up the beach slope. In doing so, the egg-laden turtle leaves behind a clear track which can be used to identify her species. *Chelonia*, *Natator*, and *Dermochelys* move their foreflippers forward simultaneously, literally "dragging" themselves up the beach. They leave behind a symmetrical track where the front flippers create diagonal grooves on the sides of the track and the hind flippers gouge paired mounds down the center of the track. *Eretmochelys*, *Caretta*, and *Lepidochelys* alternate their gait; that is, one front flipper moves forward at the same time as the hind flipper on the opposite side, leaving behind an asymmetrical ("zipper") track with offset flipper marks. The ballpark width of the track can also be used to identify the species:

Average Width of Turtle Tracks

Symmetrical Tracks		Asymmetrical Tracks	
Black	70 - 90 cm	Kemp's Ridley	70 - 80 cm
Flatback	90 cm	Olive Ridley	70 - 80 cm
Green	100 - 130 cm	Hawksbill	70 - 85 cm
Leatherback	150 - 230+ cm	Loggerhead	80 - 90+ cm

Stages of Successful Loggerhead Nesting

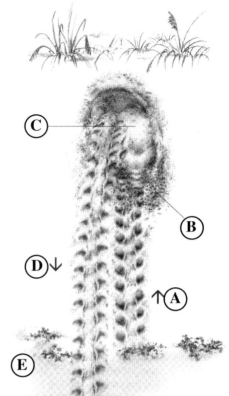

Besides identifying a specific turtle species, careful observation of tracks can often reveal the various stages of nesting, and whether or not eggs were successfully laid.

A. Emerging crawl.
B. Sand misted or thrown back over the emerging track.
C. A secondary body pit and escarpment, with sand thrown in the vicinity.
D. Returning crawl.
E. Marks the high tide line.

Source: Dawn Witherington *in* Schroeder and Murphy (1999). Used with permission.

Examples of False Crawls (Non-Nesting Emergences) Made by Loggerhead Sea Turtles

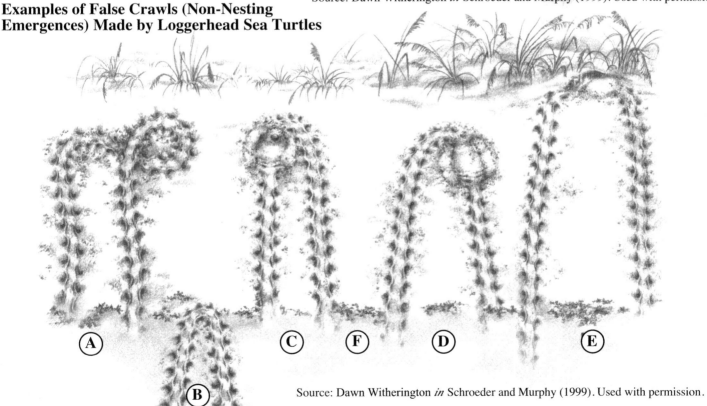

Source: Dawn Witherington *in* Schroeder and Murphy (1999). Used with permission.

A. Extensive wandering with no body pitting or digging.
B. U-shaped crawl to the high tide line (no attempt to nest).
C. Considerable sand disturbance, evidence of body pitting and digging with a smooth-walled egg chamber, but no evidence of covering.
D. Considerable sand disturbance and evidence of body pitting and digging, but no evidence of covering.
E. Marks the site of a crawl where the relative lengths of the emerging and returning crawls are the same.
F. Marks the high tide line.

Egg Laying

Most species undergo lengthy migrations from prime feeding areas to distant or isolated nesting beaches, and back again. Using satellite telemetry, scientists are now able to show that turtles can maintain straight courses in the open ocean over long distances and even keep their bearings while crossing the equator. The precise mechanism for this is unknown, but turtles probably use a variety of cues to stay on course through what we might consider to be a vast and featureless ocean expanse. These cues most likely include current patterns, the earth's magnetic field, and seasonal changes in ambient light and temperature. In the case of leatherbacks, long-term studies using satellite telemetry demonstrate that 10,000 miles or more may be traveled every year and that these travels include tropical nesting destinations every 2-5 years.

Females nest during seasons that are most conducive to the successful incubation of eggs. In general, these are the warmest and/or driest months of the year. Sea turtles will deposit anywhere from 1 to 12 clutches of eggs per nesting season, with an average, depending on the species, of 3 to 6 clutches. Most sea turtles show strong nest site association, often returning to the exact same nesting beach for many consecutive nestings and repeating the pattern for two decades or more.

After egg-laying is complete, the female will leave behind her offspring and re-enter the ocean. There is no parental care in sea turtles.

© David Schriechte

Nocturnal nesting confers several advantages, including reducing the probability of predation for both the female and her eggs. But whether a sea turtle nests during the day or night appears to be, in part, a function of size. A large turtle that came ashore to nest during the day would be leaving behind its major overheating protection – the water. On land, sunlight hitting a large sea turtle expending high amounts of energy digging, and later covering and disguising, a nest could cause a rapid and potentially lethal increase in internal body temperature. Even under non-lethal conditions, a large turtle nesting during the day might not be able to complete nesting due to heat stress. The smallest species (the Kemp's and olive ridleys), on the other hand, do tend to nest during the day. Day or night, tidal level may also play a role; coming ashore during a high tide reduces the amount of time needed to reach a nest site that won't be inundated by tidal waters.

© Scott A. Eckert

© Scott A. Eckert

Why Cover The Eggs?
1. Protects them from predators.
2. Protects them from drying out.
3. Minimizes temperature fluctuation.

© Scott A. Eckert

What Makes a Good Nest Site?

In many places, human take and sale of eggs have severely affected what in pre-modern times were highly productive nesting beaches.

1. Beach area must be accessible from the sea.
2. Angle of beach must be high enough, or the nest set back far enough, so that high tide won't routinely inundate the eggs.
3. Site must be high enough to prevent the underlying water table from reaching the nest (otherwise the embryos will drown).
4. The nesting substrate must be moist enough to prevent collapse during construction of the egg chamber.
5. The nesting substrate must be porous enough to allow gas diffusion during incubation.

The end result is an incubating habitat in which the eggs develop in a relatively high humidity, low salinity, well-ventilated environment.

© Robert Thorn

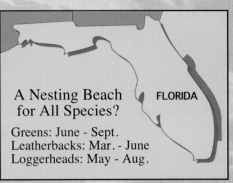

A Nesting Beach for All Species? FLORIDA

Greens: June - Sept.
Leatherbacks: Mar. - June
Loggerheads: May - Aug.

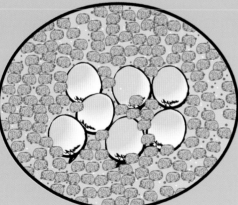

Green sea turtles dig a single body pit, about 1 meter long by 1 meter wide

Unlike chicken eggs, sea turtle eggs have no air pocket in them; the embryo attaches itself to the inside of the egg shell and breathes directly through the porous shell membrane.

Leatherback sea turtles, sometimes weighing more than a ton, leave an impressive nest site characterized by "hills and valleys" that might span 10 m or more in diameter.

© Scott A. Eckert

The Nest Environment

Oxygen
Carbon Dioxde

Water (Moisture)

T

Sand Granule Size Too Small   **Optimal Sand Granule Size**

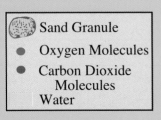

Sand Granule
Oxygen Molecules
Carbon Dioxide Molecules
Water

The properties of the sand (color, composition, compaction, etc.) surrounding the nest are important in determining how moist the nest environment can remain over time. Moisture levels in the nest can be critical in maintaining the appropriate temperature, humidity, salinity and gas exchange necessary for embryo development. Another consideration in optimizing the nesting environment is sand granule size. Because the eggs will be surrounded on all sides by sand grains, gases that normally would diffuse in and out of the egg may be inhibited by a sand grain barrier. The smaller the grains, the less open space, and therefore less space will be available for gas diffusion between the embryo (through the egg shell) and the nest.

Why So Many Eggs?

Sea turtles lay an unusually large number of eggs for a reptile. The number laid is an evolutionary compromise between:

- Energy (both for her own survival, and how much she can invest in each egg),
- Physiological capabilities and geometric capacity (e.g. available space inside her for egg production),
- Hatchling requirements (too few hatchlings could not escape from the depths of the sandy nest),
- Survivorship (predation and other factors affecting the number of young that will mature into adulthood).

© David Schrichte

The only parental care provided by sea turtles is the female's choice of a nesting site and the effort she puts into creating and then re-filling and disguising her nest. Once the nest site is selected, the female digs a **body pit** through use of both her fore and hindflippers; this involves clearing aside the dry surface sand so it doesn't sift back into the nest. After creating this depression, she positions her body within it and uses her hind flippers to excavate an **egg chamber** into which she will deposit her **clutch** of eggs. The depth of this chamber will be determined by the angle of the turtle's body in the **body pit** and the length of the turtle's hind flippers. Depending on species, female turtles will lay anywhere from 50 to 200 or more perfectly round eggs. Eggs are laid singly or in small groups and are surrounded by a thick mucus which, along with

their soft leathery shell, helps to cushion the drop and protect the developing embryos from the elements (both biological and physical). During egg-laying, the female is less cognizant of her surroundings than is the case during other phases of nesting. She does not defend the eggs against predators or poachers, and will cover the nest even if all of the eggs have been consumed by small mammals or collected by humans.

After laying her **clutch** the female will use her hind flippers to cover the nest with sand and compact it. Females typically lay multiple **clutches** within a single breeding season. This helps to ensure that at least some eggs will survive potential nest disturbances, and that a sufficient number of young will survive to maturity (which takes a really long time in sea turtles).

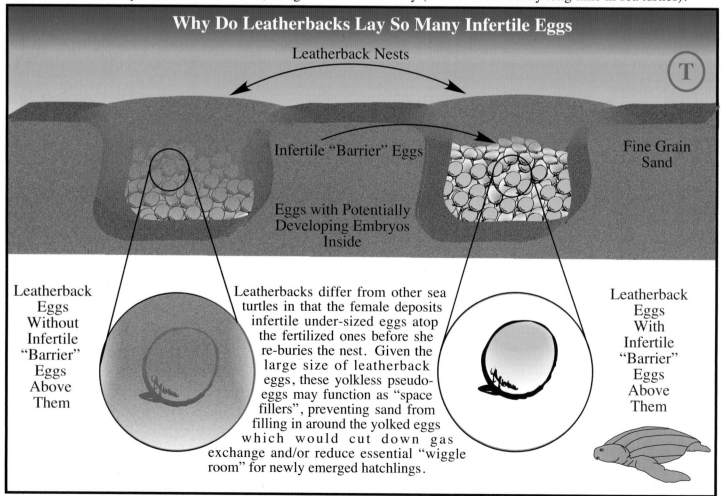

Why Do Leatherbacks Lay So Many Infertile Eggs

Leatherback Nests

Infertile "Barrier" Eggs

Fine Grain Sand

Eggs with Potentially Developing Embryos Inside

(T)

Leatherback Eggs Without Infertile "Barrier" Eggs Above Them

Leatherbacks differ from other sea turtles in that the female deposits infertile under-sized eggs atop the fertilized ones before she re-buries the nest. Given the large size of leatherback eggs, these yolkless pseudo-eggs may function as "space fillers", preventing sand from filling in around the yolked eggs which would cut down gas exchange and/or reduce essential "wiggle room" for newly emerged hatchlings.

Leatherback Eggs With Infertile "Barrier" Eggs Above Them

Sea Turtle Mass Nestings: Arribadas

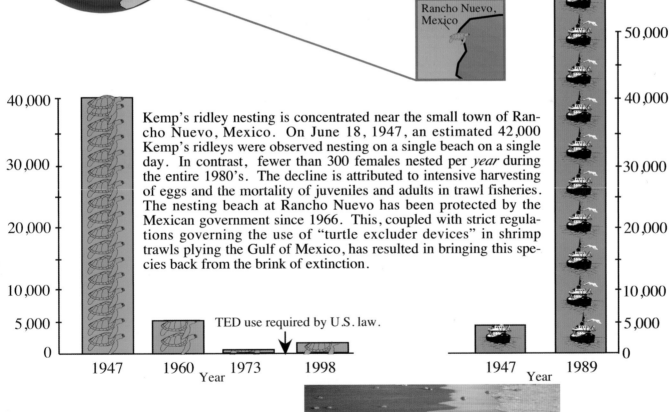

Some turtles show multiple nesting strategies: solitary (seen by all species) and aggregated (or mass) nestings. Kemp's ridley and olive ridley turtles go through mass nesting behaviors where literally thousands of females may come ashore to lay eggs at the same time. This unique nesting event is called an **arribada** from the Spanish term for "arrival". Often it appears correlated with moon or tidal phases, although its precise impetus is unclear.

© Stephen Cornelius

Rancho Nuevo, Mexico

Kemp's ridley nesting is concentrated near the small town of Rancho Nuevo, Mexico. On June 18, 1947, an estimated 42,000 Kemp's ridleys were observed nesting on a single beach on a single day. In contrast, fewer than 300 females nested per *year* during the entire 1980's. The decline is attributed to intensive harvesting of eggs and the mortality of juveniles and adults in trawl fisheries. The nesting beach at Rancho Nuevo has been protected by the Mexican government since 1966. This, coupled with strict regulations governing the use of "turtle excluder devices" in shrimp trawls plying the Gulf of Mexico, has resulted in bringing this species back from the brink of extinction.

Number of Nesting Female Kemp's Ridleys at Rancho Nuevo

40,000
30,000
20,000
10,000
5,000
0

TED use required by U.S. law.

1947   1960   1973   1998
Year

Number of U.S. Shrimp Trawlers in Gulf of Mexico

50,000
40,000
30,000
20,000
10,000
5,000
0

1947   1989
Year

Olive ridleys coming ashore at Nancite, Costa Rica. Other major arribada sites for the olive ridley occur in India (both east and west coasts), Pacific Mexico, northern Australia, Mozambique, and selected sites in Western Africa and the Guianas.

© Stephen Cornelius

Sex Determination

Unlike many animals, a sea turtle's sex is not determined at the time of conception, but instead is greatly influenced by the temperature of the sand in the nest where the egg lies.

Importantly, global warming might result in changes to the incubation environment, resulting in skewed sex ratios, decreased hatch success, and/or the loss of sandy beach habitat.

Major Factors Affecting Clutch Temperature

- Beach Temperature

- Heat Exchange Between Clutch & Beach

Sea turtles lack sex chromosomes, meaning that whether a hatchling is a boy or a girl is not decided at the time of fertilization (as is the case with humans), but rather it is during incubation that sex determination occurs. Individual egg incubation temperature is thought to play the critical role in whether a hatchling emerges from the nest as a male or a female. In general, warmer temperatures produce females while cooler temperatures produce males. This phenomenon, called TSD (or Temperature-dependent Sex Determination) by those in the turtle sex business, has critical implications when it comes to human impacts and the success of certain types of conservation efforts (see page 108). As you can imagine, entirely natural factors can affect incubation temperatures in such a way as to result in a seasonal production of primarily males or females. Likewise, an egg's individual position within a nest might be critical to whether it becomes a male or a female; eggs positioned within the center of the nest are more insulated and also may receive additional heat emanating from adjacent eggs, potentially increasing the odds on them becoming females. Humans can influence the system in a number of ways, such as by clearing beach vegetation and removing natural shading.

The sensitive time during incubation, when the egg is most susceptible to temperature affecting sexual determination, appears to be during the middle third of the incubation period.

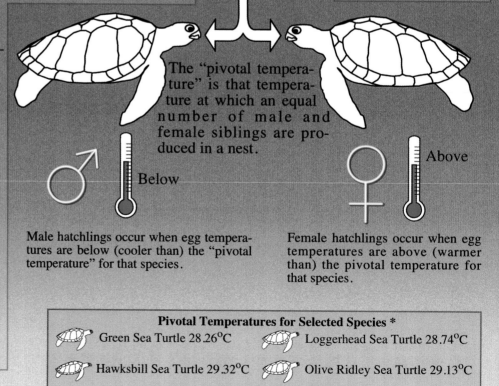

The "pivotal temperature" is that temperature at which an equal number of male and female siblings are produced in a nest.

Below

Above

Male hatchlings occur when egg temperatures are below (cooler than) the "pivotal temperature" for that species.

Female hatchlings occur when egg temperatures are above (warmer than) the pivotal temperature for that species.

Pivotal Temperatures for Selected Species *

Green Sea Turtle 28.26°C		Loggerhead Sea Turtle 28.74°C	
Hawksbill Sea Turtle 29.32°C		Olive Ridley Sea Turtle 29.13°C	

*varies by geographic region; data from Ackerman, 1997.

The Importance of Sea Turtles as Biological Transporters of Energy and Nutrients into Relatively Nutrient-Poor Beach Environments

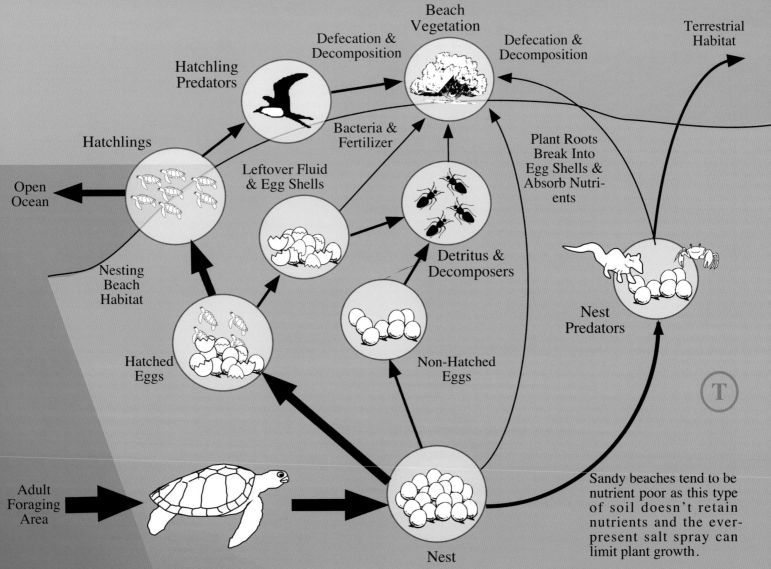

The thickness of each arrow represents the relative energy amount and direction of movement.

The introduction of nutrients and energy from outside ecosystems can be extremely important in nutrient-stressed atoll coastal habitats and beach dune areas where the majority of sea turtle nesting occurs. This is primarily due to the relatively low biological diversity and primary productivity associated with these sediment habitats. Often the inputs into these systems come from wave or wind action driving carrion, algal wrack or surf diatoms ashore, or through rain runoff from the terrestrial side. Two potentially important biological sources of nutrients and energy are migratory seabirds and sea turtles in these areas. Female sea turtles can carry both nutrients and energy from foraging areas hundreds or even thousands of miles away, where it's later deposited as eggs in the nest she leaves behind on the sandy shore. The energy and nutrients now represented by the developing embryos, amniotic fluids and egg shells can follow a number of paths that will end up exiting the immediate habitat as either hatchlings entering the ocean or through the actions of predators. At the other end of the spectrum, energy and nutrients can also remain in the habitat through the localized food web and end up incorporated into predators, detritivores, and decomposers, which in turn may re-deposit such energy and nutrients into the primary producers, the beach vegetation, resulting in increased plant growth and dune stabilization. As a result, the dune plant community is able to support increased faunal densities (including herbivorous insects and birds) and offers greater protection against habitat loss due to physical actions, such as storms. By stabilizing the beach dune environment, the turtles may be contributing to their future reproductive success by ensuring an appropriate nesting habitat!

Modified after Bouchard & Bjorndal (2000).

Hatchlings

The Life of a Hatchling

Hatchlings use a **caruncle**, a specialized egg tooth, to help break free of the egg shell which had been their home during early development. The **caruncle** disappears shortly after hatching. Once the hatchling breaks free of its shell, it begins the long process of digging its way to the surface. Movement caused by breaking free of the eggshell elicits such behavior in adjacent unhatched eggs. As more and more hatchlings break out of their shells, their digging stimulates digging by siblings and together they endeavor to reach the surface in a rare display of social facilitation that scientists call protocooperation (see page 72). This process continues until the mass of hatchlings is right beneath the surface, at which point the intense heat of the surface sand (assuming it's daylight) essentially immobilizes them and they stop digging until the sun lowers and the sand cools. If the hatchlings

© Scott A. Eckert

approach the surface during the cool of the tropical night, they emerge directly. Once at the surface, the tiny turtles open their eyes for the first time, orient to the open horizon, and scurry to the sea. Making a run for it at night may be selective not only because of lower surface sand temperatures, but also decreased predation risk both on the beach and in nearshore waters.

The trek to the sea is not as straightforward as you might think. To a hatchling, a single person's footprint on the beach can be a serious obstacle to be overcome in its quest to reach the water. Vehicle tracks, landscaping, sailboats, logs, marine debris and even the lounging bodies of snoring tourists atop beach towels can serve as impenetrable barriers. Physical obstacles are not the only threat. Lights on a beach where hatchlings are emerging can disorient and misdirect the young turtles, preventing them from reaching the sea. Over millions of years, hatchlings have evolved a strong sensitivity to the subtle brightness of the open ocean horizon (as opposed to a relatively darker beach or dune profile). This carefully honed spectral sensitivity gives the newborns their strongest clue as to the location of their intended destination – the sea.

© Scott A. Eckert

Protocooperation

After the hatchling breaks through the eggshell, the various fluids drain away, creating an individual air space. As more and more eggs hatch, a volume of shared air space surrounds the emerging hatchlings, who, stimulated by jostling and hatching siblings on all sides and instinctively aware of which direction is "up", start to wiggle and dig towards the surface in a rare example of cooperation among individuals. The hatchlings move upwards as a group through the sand. The shared air space moves with them, as sand is moved from above to fill the empty chamber space below. This act of social facilitation (also referred to as Protocooperation) results in the majority of the hatchlings reaching the surface at once. The journey to the surface is a difficult one, and may require several days to complete. The hatchlings work in bouts, relying on spurts of energy that, once depleted, leave the little turtles quiet and resting. As a fresh supply of oxygen flows into the nest from the surrounding sand, the hatchlings are re-energized and make another spurt of progress. Once near the surface, the heat of the surface sand has an immobilizing effect on the hatchlings. This is Nature's way of keeping them from exposing themselves during the heat of the day, minimizing both predation and heat stress. In the late afternoon and early evening the sand cools quickly, and this is the primary period of hatchling emergence.

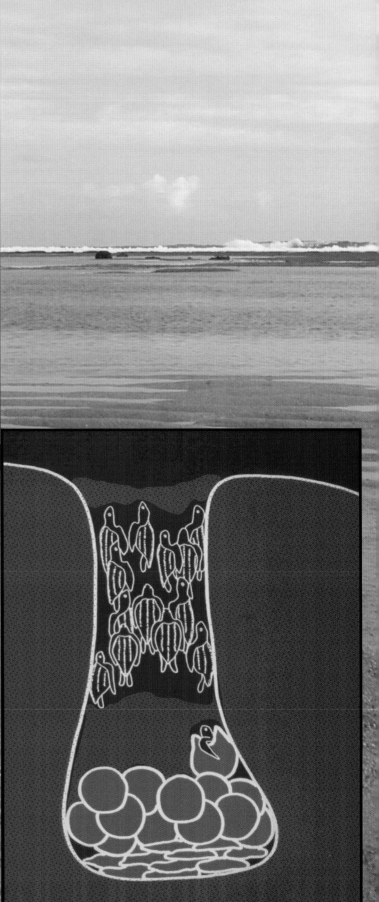

Modified from Fretey (1981). Used with permission.

From Embryo to Hatchling

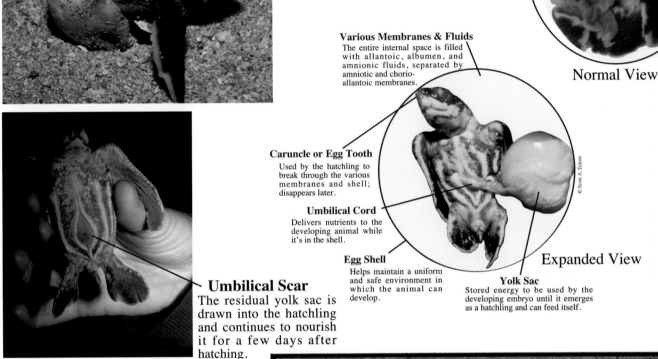

Various Membranes & Fluids
The entire internal space is filled with allantoic, albumen, and amnionic fluids, separated by amniotic and chorio-allantoic membranes.

Normal View

Caruncle or Egg Tooth
Used by the hatchling to break through the various membranes and shell; disappears later.

Umbilical Cord
Delivers nutrients to the developing animal while it's in the shell.

Egg Shell
Helps maintain a uniform and safe environment in which the animal can develop.

Expanded View

Yolk Sac
Stored energy to be used by the developing embryo until it emerges as a hatchling and can feed itself.

Umbilical Scar
The residual yolk sac is drawn into the hatchling and continues to nourish it for a few days after hatching.

The type of coloration seen in a hatchling/juvenile provides a clue as to where it spends the "lost years" of its earliest life. Most hatchlings (and the resulting juveniles) show some form of counter-shading, which is thought to help protect them from both aerial (seabirds) and sub-surface predators. To predators in the air, the turtle hatchling blends in with the darker waters below; to predators underneath, the lighter underside of the hatchling helps it blend in with the down-welling light from the surface. Counter-shading is most pronounced in green sea turtles, with the hatchling having a distinctive black dorsal color and a bright white ventral color.

Many hatchlings also have some form of ridges along their backs which are thought to improve laminar flow, allowing them to smoothly and efficiently swim through the water for sustained periods.

Dorsal (Top) Side

Hawksbill   Green   Leatherback

COUNTERSHADING

Ventral (Bottom) Side

How Do Hatchlings Navigate From the Nest to the Open Ocean?

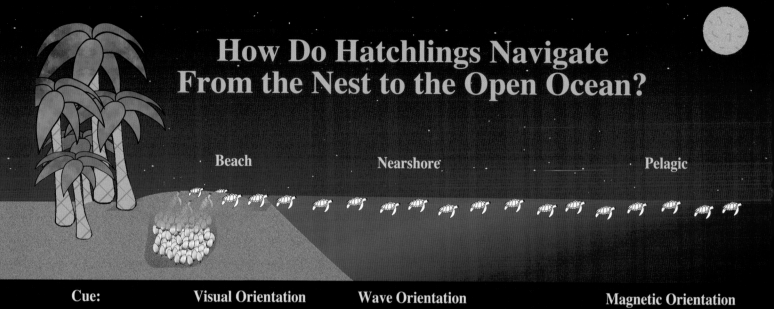

Beach **Nearshore** **Pelagic**

Cue: **Visual Orientation** **Wave Orientation** **Magnetic Orientation**

Visual cues (what the hatchlings actually see with their eyes) guide hatchlings from the nest site to the ocean's edge. When they first enter the water they rely on an unusual ability scientists refer to as a "wave compass", orienting directly against the incoming wave surge in order to maintain an open sea bearing. As they get farther out to sea, laboratory research supports the hypothesis that turtles switch to use of a "magnetic compass", perhaps facilitated by **magnetite** within their brains, in order to maintain their direction. For many vertebrates, use of a magnetic compass for orientation has been shown to involve modulating the response of the retinal photoreceptors to light; interestingly, leatherback hatchlings use geomagnetic orientation in complete darkness. The end result is that like their distant cousins the birds, turtles appear to use a combination of environmental cues and internal compasses to help them migrate.

© Scott A. Eckert

Swim Frenzy!

When the hatchlings reach the water, their crawling form of locomotion is replaced by "dog-paddling". They may be thrown back ashore by strong waves more than once, but persistence wins the day and soon the hatchlings are in a run for their lives through a gauntlet of predator fishes and seabirds. This "swim frenzy" may last for several days and, in general, is designed to carry the hatchlings into open ocean current gyres that serve as nursery grounds.

The Lost Years

Termed the "lost years" because the very youngest sea turtle life stages were not seen by early sea turtle researchers. Today scientists know that the "lost years", sometimes more like a "lost decade", are spent adrift in ocean currents where the young turtles are feeding mainly in **driftlines** and other accumulations of debris that also afford some protective camouflage. The loggerhead, for example, is perfectly colored at this stage (brown and tan) for hiding amongst the large drift algae that makes up the "Sargasso Sea" in the central Atlantic.

While at sea, baby turtles sleep or rest at the surface with their front flippers tucked up over their backs; this has the effect of decreasing the profile they provide to potential predators and minimizes limb exposure to beasties looking for a late night snack.

The exceptions to the "lost years" scenario may be the flatback turtle, which is thought to remain in Australian coastal waters after its initial swim frenzy, and the leatherback, which spends much of its life on the high seas. Only recently, with the help of satellite telemetry, have scientists been able to glimpse the remarkable migrations and fascinating lifestyle of this reclusive reptile for which only a relative handful of **juveniles** have ever been seen.

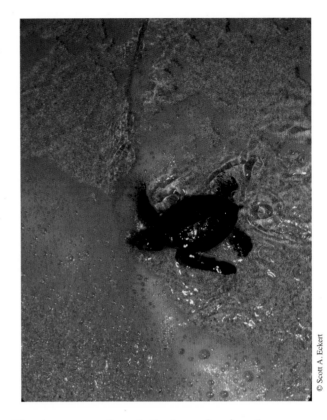

© Scott A. Eckert

Having completed their **pelagic** phase, most young turtles "re-appear" when they're about the size of a dinner plate. These animals recruit to coastal feeding areas where they reside until they reach sexual maturity. It should be noted that this is often a highly mobile stage of a sea turtle's life, and a "coastal feeding area" may embrace the territorial waters of dozens of nations. The passage from juvenile to "sub-adult" to sexually mature adult may take an additional 15 to 30 years after the young turtle leaves its earliest high seas nursery habitat to begin life as a more typically coastal species.

© Scott A. Eckert

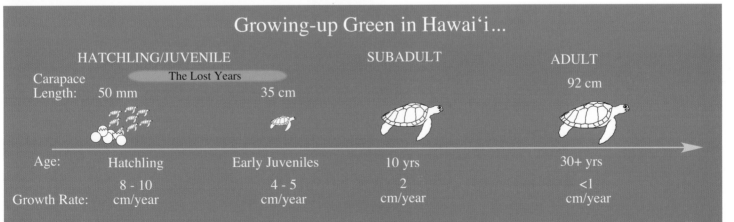

Growing-up Green in Hawai'i...

	HATCHLING/JUVENILE		SUBADULT	ADULT
Carapace Length:	50 mm	The Lost Years 35 cm		92 cm
Age:	Hatchling	Early Juveniles	10 yrs	30+ yrs
Growth Rate:	8 - 10 cm/year	4 - 5 cm/year	2 cm/year	<1 cm/year

The growth rate of a green sea turtle varies during different stages of its life cycle. This variation represents a trade-off between putting energy into rapid growth to achieve a size refuge from many predators and dedicating it towards reproduction. It also may reflect a change in diet as these herbivorous animals vary their geographical location with age.

Adapted from Zug *et al.*, 2002

HAWAIIAN GREEN SEA TURTLES
Life History

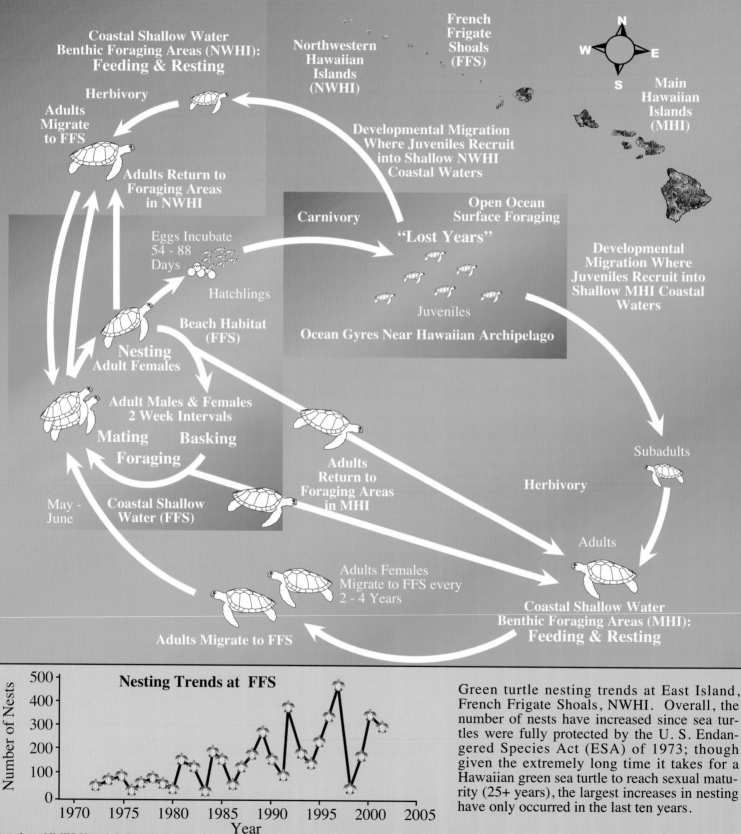

Coastal Shallow Water Benthic Foraging Areas (NWHI): **Feeding & Resting**

Herbivory

Adults Migrate to FFS

Adults Return to Foraging Areas in NWHI

Northwestern Hawaiian Islands (NWHI)

French Frigate Shoals (FFS)

Main Hawaiian Islands (MHI)

Developmental Migration Where Juveniles Recruit into Shallow NWHI Coastal Waters

Carnivory

Eggs Incubate 54 - 88 Days

Hatchlings

Beach Habitat (FFS)

Nesting Adult Females

Open Ocean Surface Foraging

"Lost Years"

Juveniles

Ocean Gyres Near Hawaiian Archipelago

Developmental Migration Where Juveniles Recruit into Shallow MHI Coastal Waters

Adult Males & Females 2 Week Intervals

Mating   Basking

Foraging

May - June

Coastal Shallow Water (FFS)

Adults Return to Foraging Areas in MHI

Herbivory

Subadults

Adults

Adults Females Migrate to FFS every 2 - 4 Years

Adults Migrate to FFS

Coastal Shallow Water Benthic Foraging Areas (MHI): **Feeding & Resting**

Nesting Trends at FFS

Number of Nests

500
400
300
200
100
0

1970   1975   1980   1985   1990   1995   2000   2005

Year

(data from NMFS Honolulu Laboratory)

Green turtle nesting trends at East Island, French Frigate Shoals, NWHI. Overall, the number of nests have increased since sea turtles were fully protected by the U. S. Endangered Species Act (ESA) of 1973; though given the extremely long time it takes for a Hawaiian green sea turtle to reach sexual maturity (25+ years), the largest increases in nesting have only occurred in the last ten years.

Natural History of the Hawaiian Green Sea Turtle

Hawaiian green sea turtles are unique among U. S. sea turtle populations in spending their entire lives within the Hawaiian Island chain. Over ninety percent of all Hawaiian green sea turtle nesting takes place on six small islets located around the lagoon at French Frigate Shoals in the middle of the Northwestern Hawaiian Islands. This area is extremely remote, and with the exception of intense fishing pressure during the 1950's and 1960's (over 25% of the nesting females were taken by a fishing company and shipped to Honolulu during 1959), has provided a necessary haven from human interference during nesting and hatching seasons.

© David Schrichte

© David Schrichte

Recently this area along with the rest of the northern portion of the archipelago was declared a Northwestern Hawaiian Islands Coral Reef Ecosystem Reserve, providing a greater level of protection for these magnificent creatures.

Primarily a solitary animal by nature, Hawaiian green sea turtles have been known to congregate around foraging pastures of algae or seagrass. Interestingly, the composition of algae in a Hawaiian green turtle's diet varies from island to island – and sometimes from one side of an island to the other!

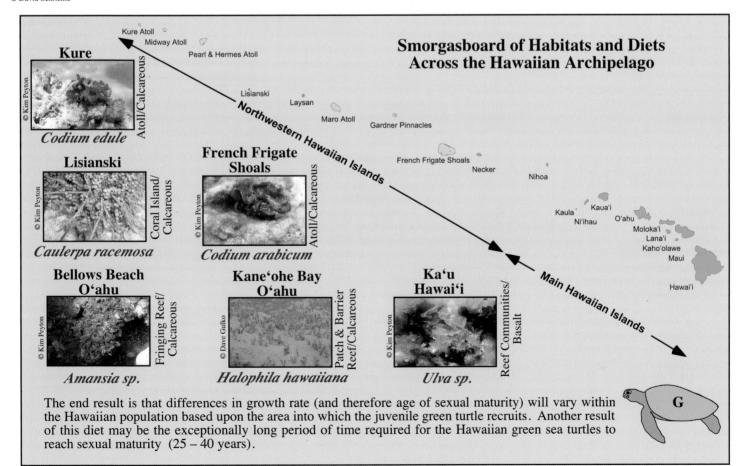

Smorgasboard of Habitats and Diets Across the Hawaiian Archipelago

Kure Atoll
Midway Atoll
Pearl & Hermes Atoll

Kure
© Kim Peyton
Codium edule
Atoll/Calcareous

Lisianski
Laysan
Maro Atoll
Gardner Pinnacles

French Frigate Shoals
Necker
Nihoa

Northwestern Hawaiian Islands

Lisianski
© Kim Peyton
Caulerpa racemosa
Coral Island/Calcareous

French Frigate Shoals
© Kim Peyton
Codium arabicum
Atoll/Calcareous

Kaula
Kaua'i
Ni'ihau
O'ahu
Moloka'i
Lana'i
Kaho'olawe
Maui
Hawai'i

Main Hawaiian Islands

Bellows Beach O'ahu
© Kim Peyton
Amansia sp.
Fringing Reef/Calcareous

Kane'ohe Bay O'ahu
© Dave Gulko
Halophila hawaiiana
Patch & Barrier Reef/Calcareous

Ka'u Hawai'i
© Kim Peyton
Ulva sp.
Reef Communities/Basalt

G

The end result is that differences in growth rate (and therefore age of sexual maturity) will vary within the Hawaiian population based upon the area into which the juvenile green turtle recruits. Another result of this diet may be the exceptionally long period of time required for the Hawaiian green sea turtles to reach sexual maturity (25 – 40 years).

Green Sea Turtles and the Coral Reef Food Web in the Northwestern Hawaiian Islands

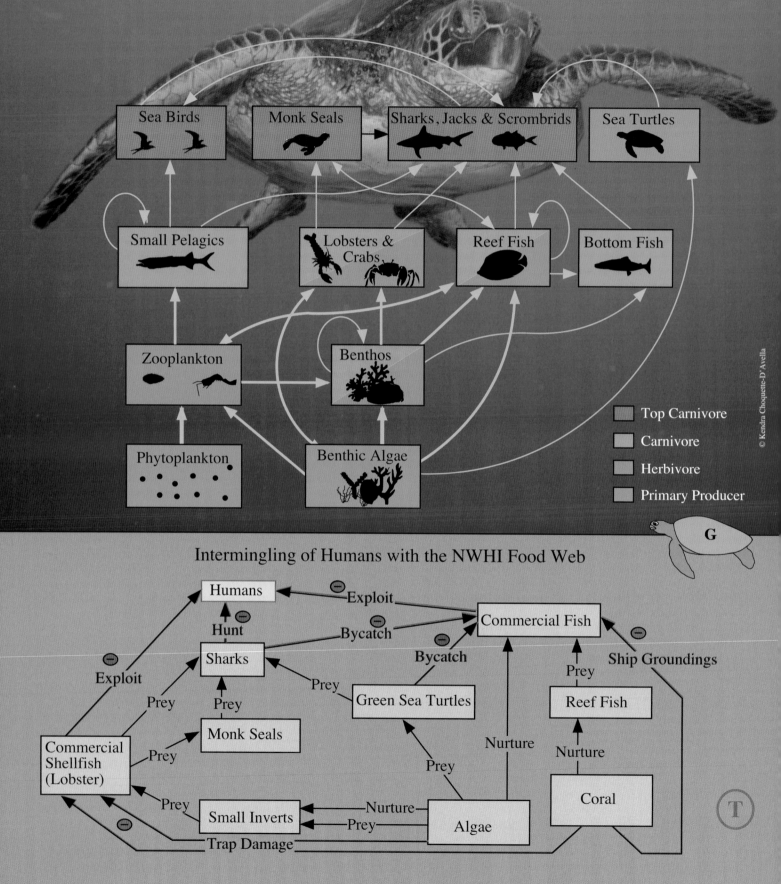

© Kendra Choquette-D'Avella

Top Carnivore
Carnivore
Herbivore
Primary Producer

Intermingling of Humans with the NWHI Food Web

THE TUMOR PROBLEM

First seen in green sea turtles in the USA (Florida and Hawai'i) in 1938, these lobed tumor growths (fibropapillomas) can range in size from an almost undetectable 0.1 cm (0.04 inches) to a whopping 30 cm (1 foot) in diameter! Tumors have now been reported in a range of sea turtle species, including loggerhead, olive ridley and flatback turtles and the disease appears to have a world-wide distribution.

Recent work has shown that tumor-like cells can appear in cells associated with the lungs, liver, intestines, kidneys and testes in addition to external skin tissue.

© Ursula Keuper-Bennett/Peter Bennett

© Ursula Keuper-Bennett/Peter Bennett

Originally spirorchid trematodes (a type of flatworm) were suspected of serving as vectors for introduction of this disease, but recent work has shown this to not be the case; though their increased presence in affected animals may be a secondary effect. Currently fibropapillomas are thought to be related to the herpes virus. Samples of green sea turtle tumor tissue were found to harbor herpesvirus DNA; additional data have shown herpes viruses associated with tumor tissues from loggerhead and olive ridley turtles.

As these growths grow over portions of the animal's flippers, neck, mouth and eyes they greatly inhibit the ability of the animal to seek shelter, feed and move about. Increased stress, including exposure to predation and human impacts, eventually takes its toll.

Other Health Problems:

A wide variety of ailments can affect in sea turtles. Bacterial mycoplasma has been found in green sea turtles where it negatively impacts muscles, the circulatory system, the liver and the spleen. A parasitic protozoan, *Caryospora cheloniae*, has been found in the lower digestive tract of green sea turtles. Olive ridleys have been captured at sea with cataracts in both eyes.

Ciguatera, caused by a single-celled dinoflagellate, *Gambiodiscus* spp., may also affect a variety of sea turtles. Humans that eat fish or turtle infected with ciguatoxin can get seriously ill or die. There are also documented cases of cholera-type diarrhea, a serious condition caused by the bacteria *Vibro mimicus* found in olive ridley turtle eggs.

Disease Detectives (What Can Simple Tests Tell Us?):

Feces: Evidence of protozoan and bacterial infections, worm infestations.
Tissue Fluids & Biopsies: Can be used to isolate and confirm viral, bacterial or fungal diseases.
Blood Work: Allows quantification of systemic bacterial infections and identification of blood-borne pathogens or parasites. Blood cell counts and plasma component analysis can be used to detect effects on other organs such as the kidneys, liver and muscles. Antibody tests conducted on blood samples can detect the presence of antigens from specific diseases.
DNA Work: New techniques involving nucleic acid probes and primers can shed light on bacterial and fungal diseases common to a variety of animals.

Sites of Fibropapilloma Cutaneous & Visceral Lesions

Can affect ability to feed, navigate, and avoid predators.

EYES

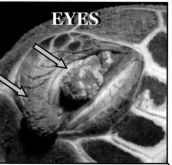

Can affect ability to filter urine, can lead to kidney disease.

KIDNEYS

Can affect ability to pump blood, can lead to cardiac arrest.

HEART

Can affect ability to reproduce, defecate, move, and steer.

BASE OF TAIL

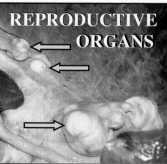

CHIN

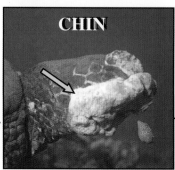

Can affect ability to feed, navigate.

REPRODUCTIVE ORGANS

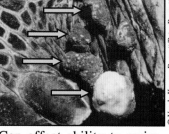

Can affect ability to produce, store, and deliver eggs and sperm.

NECK

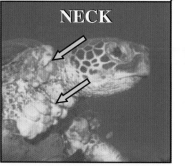

Can affect ability to move head, feed, and be aware of surroundings.

LUNGS

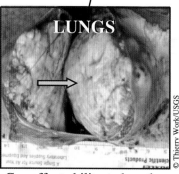

Can affect ability to breathe, can lead to pneumonia.

LIVER

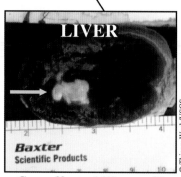
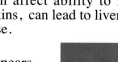

Can affect ability to filter toxins, can lead to liver disease.

FLIPPER

Can affect ability to swim, migrate, feed, and predator avoidance.

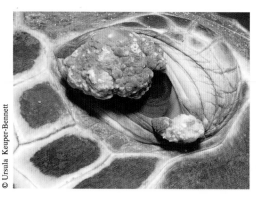

Internally, this disease appears to spread primarily through the circulatory system, where it can affect a wide variety of body functions.

As of 1998, scientists estimated that over 65% of the green turtles in Kane'ohe Bay, Hawai'i and up to 35% of the greens off the Hawaiian island of Moloka'i were afflicted.

NATURAL THREATS

Nest inundation or loss to erosion due to heavy rains or high tides can cause nest failure, as can the accretion of additional sand atop the nest due to natural beach processes. Unusual heat or cold, root growth, and bacterial invasions also pose threats.

Nest washout by storm waves.

A wide variety of natural predators prey on eggs and hatchlings, including crabs, ants (see photo above), lizards, seabirds, vultures, and raccoons. Once the hatchlings hit the water, they are eaten by seabirds, sharks and other predatory fish such as catfish and jacks. However, because native predatory species play an important role in coastal ecosystems, their removal is discouraged in favor of nest protection and other turtle-saving strategies. On the other hand, the controlled removal non-native species (or native species whose populations are artificially elevated due to human settlement) can be healthy for the ecology of coastal nesting areas.

Vultures eating leatherback hatchlings.

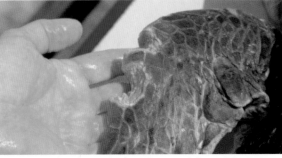

Incomplete predation by mahi mahi on a green turtle.

Feral animals and unleashed pets are not part of the natural eco-systems associated with the life history of sea turtles. Because popula-tions of feral organisms are often a direct result of human settlement and activity, they are not considered a "natur-al stress" but instead a human-associated threat to sea turtle survival. Thousands of hatch-lings are eaten by roam-ing dogs on a nightly basis at some sites.

© Scott A. Eckert

© Scott A. Eckert

How A Series of Natural Stresses Can Lead to Loss of an Entire Nest

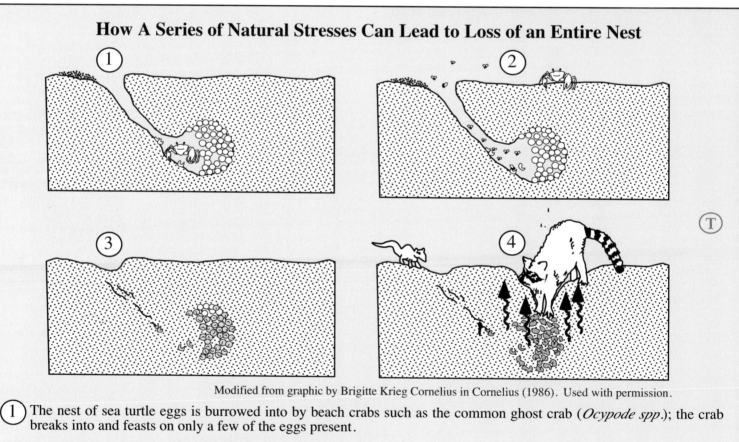

Modified from graphic by Brigitte Krieg Cornelius in Cornelius (1986). Used with permission.

① The nest of sea turtle eggs is burrowed into by beach crabs such as the common ghost crab (*Ocypode spp.*); the crab breaks into and feasts on only a few of the eggs present.

② The ghost crab moves on, abandoning the invaded nest. Flies (*Asyndetus spp.*) enter the burrowed opening and lay their eggs amongst the broken turtle eggs.

③ The fly eggs hatch and the hungry larval grubs feed on the decaying contents of the broken turtle eggs that had been previously feasted upon by the ghost crab; the larvae also crawl around and atop the healthy eggs in the nest. Fungus brought in by the flies and inoculated onto the decaying eggs is now spread to healthy, intact eggs through the activi-ties of the larval grubs. As the fungus spreads over the shells of healthy eggs, it leads to a cessation of embryo devel-opment, possibly through inhibition of gas exchange across the eggshell barrier.

④ As the majority of eggs and embryos in the nest start to decay, the resulting stench rises up through airspaces in the sand, eventually reaching the beach surface where the odor serves to attract small mammals to the site. Their digging into the nest exposes any remaining live embryos to predation, and the nest is lost.

Strategies to Minimize Nest Looting

Protective Screens

At some sites on the southeast coast of the U. S., 80% or more of loggerhead sea turtle nests may be destroyed by raccoons. Control efforts sometimes involve the creation of physical barriers that inhibit or prevent digging by raccoons, while not interfering with egg and hatchling development. By securing treated (galvanized or plastic-coated) wire screens over buried nests, the eggs are protected from predators such as raccoons without the need for removal of the predator; in essence, a more ecosystem-friendly approach to management of this problem. Other strategies include behavioral modification (see below), removal of problem raccoons, relocation of eggs or disguising nests by masking the odors associated with them.

Non-lethal Conditioned Taste Aversion (CTA)

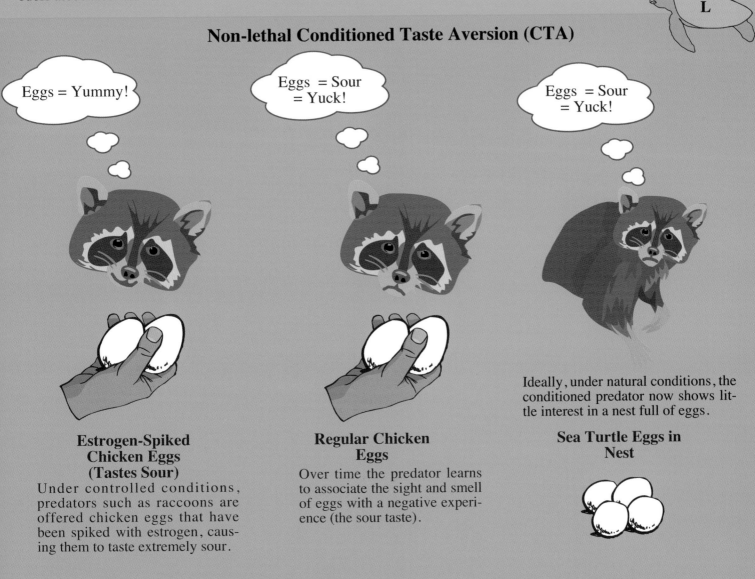

Estrogen-Spiked Chicken Eggs (Tastes Sour)

Under controlled conditions, predators such as raccoons are offered chicken eggs that have been spiked with estrogen, causing them to taste extremely sour.

Regular Chicken Eggs

Over time the predator learns to associate the sight and smell of eggs with a negative experience (the sour taste).

Ideally, under natural conditions, the conditioned predator now shows little interest in a nest full of eggs.

Sea Turtle Eggs in Nest

HUMAN-ASSOCIATED STRESSES

Let's face it, many of the reasons sea turtles are endangered have to do with how we as humans treat and use both marine and coastal environments. As we've already seen, sea turtles lay large numbers of eggs as an evolutionary strategy to deal with, among other things, very low natural survival rates of offspring; perhaps one in a thousand survives to be an adult. When human impacts are factored into the equation, survival rates may plummet, ... resulting in once thriving populations teetering on the edge of extinction.

Human-associated threats can be either direct (done intentionally) or indirect (non-intentional, accidental). In the United States, the vast majority of important threats are indirect; for example, incidental capture (bycatch) by commercial fisheries or the disorientation of hatchlings by coastal lighting. By comparison, the direct take of eggs and adults for food is a relatively minor threat (and is illegal) in the U.S. because of the protection conferred upon sea turtles by the federal Endangered Species Act.

Artificial Lighting

© Scott A. Eckert

Photopollution, or the presence of detrimental artificial light in the environment, can be disorienting to nesting females and lethal to recently emerged hatchlings. Sea turtles use subtle visual cues (related to the comparative brightness, under natural conditions, of the open ocean horizon) to orient down the beach to the surf line. Lights from roadways and vehicles, homes and restaurants, tennis courts and playing fields, condos, hotels and even beachgoers can mislead hatchlings, causing them to use precious energy stores wandering around on land and often leading them away from the ocean. Studies have shown that even distant light sources can cause problems for photo-sensitive hatchlings.

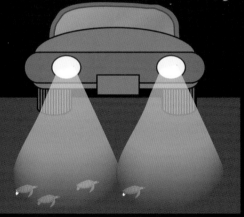
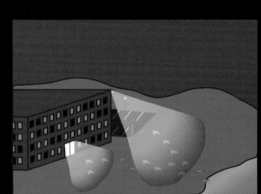

© Scott A. Eckert

The best way to deal with this problem is to eliminate light sources on beaches during nesting and hatching periods. When this is not possible, modifying human behaviors in the immediate area to limit light use during these periods can also be effective, as can lowering and shielding light sources, use of timers/motion-sensors, and replacing high intensity streetlights and security lights with low pressure sodium vapor lights that are known to be less attractive to some species of sea turtles.

Beach/Coastal Alteration

Beach enrichment ("nourishment"), seawall construction or armoring, coastal development, beach cleaning machines, and other forms of human development and use, can all result in interference with nesting activities.

Enrichment introduces sand from external sources (often dredged from nearshore deposits), typically to rebuild an eroding beach. In so doing, enrichment can alter specific characteristics of the beach (organic content, grain size, compaction qualities) and reduce its suitability as an incubating environment. For example, enrichment projects that result in highly compacted beach sediments may negatively affect turtle digging behavior, making the construction of a nest cavity impossible, or alter the incubation temperature or moisture levels in the nest (see pages 64 - 68).

Coastal armoring, on the other hand, generally involves the strategic placement of a barricade (anything from a small seawall to a substantial rock revetment) designed to protect beachfront property from wave action. In addition to directly preventing female sea turtles from reaching prime nesting habitat, such structures can actually exacerbate erosion. And by interrupting the natural movements of sand and sediments along the coast, these structures can have far-ranging effects on patterns of sea turtle nesting and foraging.

Degradation of coastal areas may also indirectly affect turtles by altering the availability of their prey. Patterns of coastal construction can affect nearshore currents, for example, which may change algae abundance or distribution. Similar changes could occur throughout all **trophic levels**, affecting the numbers and types of invertebrate and fish prey available.

As more and more people develop and live along coastal areas it is becoming increasingly difficult to find unused sandy beaches. Even undeveloped beaches can be significantly altered by recreational activities. Movement and piling of sand by children building sandcastles can create impenetrable barriers to hatchlings trying to reach the surface. Beach umbrellas penetrate the sand, puncturing eggs in their nests. Keep in mind that one doesn't need to break more than a couple eggs to create an environment where the broken eggs rot and infect the others (see page 82). Lounge chairs, sail boats and other recreational equipment, left on the beach at night, can block

access to nesting habitat. Vehicles ridden by 'joyriding' tourists tear up the beach, compact the sand, crush eggs and create deep ruts that trap emerging hatchlings. Another concern regarding compaction is that it decreases the amount of space between sand granules (see page 65), thereby decreasing the amount of space for air (oxygen) to circulate and potentially suffocating the developing embryos.

A related concern regarding coastal development and alteration is the possibility that turtles will be forced into marginal habitats. This can result in lowered nest success (due to unfavorable conditions) or lead to an unnatural concentration of nests, resulting in an increased number of disturbed and destroyed clutches of eggs as turtles unintentionally dig up nests laid earlier.

Finally, nearshore dredging, used to create deeper harbors and marinas, to keep shipping channels clear, and to extend the coastline in land-poor islands through use of fill material, can also pose a risk to sea turtles and the habitats they use. The U. S. Government strongly restricts the use of certain types of dredges in certain areas due to their ability to injure or kill sea turtles.

Boating

© Scott A. Eckert

Propeller strikes and vessel collisions can cause severe head and body lacerations. As recreational boating and marine tourism activities increase, the potential for sea turtle injury from these activities also increases. Strong concerns exist over the use of personal thrill craft, for example. In some cases, repetitive boat injuries may be caused in part by the physical or physiological consequences (affecting buoyancy, movement or vision) of the initial strike.

© Ursula Keuper-Bennett/Peter Bennett

Loggerhead recovering at the Topsail Turtle Hospital in North Carolina after being struck by a boat propeller. The material on the carapace was developed to help human burn victims, and is now helping to hold medicines in place and shattered shell fragments together. This animal survived after days of medical treatment and intensive care - many others aren't so lucky.

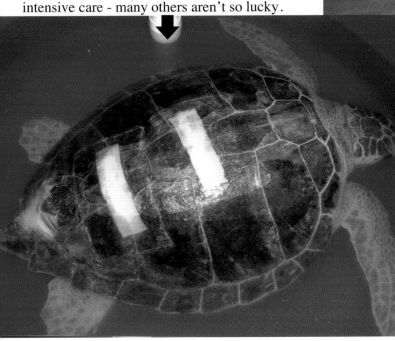

© Topsail Turtle Hospital

Dave Gulko

The advent of personal thrill craft has allowed affordable high speed vehicles to become more prevalent. Such craft can operate at high speed in very shallow waters where turtles may be feeding, mating or resting, increasing the opportunity for accidents. Some areas and jurisdictions, including marine parks, are setting an example for others to follow by taking steps to strongly curb the use of such craft in areas where sea turtles congregate.

One study showed 80% of East Pacific green turtle deaths in waters off San Diego, California, to have been associated with evidence of boat collisions.

Fishing

© David Schrichte

Perhaps the greatest threat to juvenile and adult sea turtles world wide is their incidental capture during fishing activities; with trawling, longline fishing, driftnets, lobster and fish trap lines, and gillnets causing the most damage. The result is often death by drowning due to forced submergence following entanglement within the gear. Discarded or lost fishing gear also contributes to this problem through ingestion, entanglement, or blocking of access to feeding, nesting and basking areas (see Marine Debris, page 95).

The ingestion of fishing hooks can cause severe damage to the digestive system of sea turtles, especially the esophagus; removal of such hooks can be extremely difficult (see Pelagic Fishing Effects, page 91). Even if the line is cut to free the turtle, the turtle swims away with a hook still lodged in its mouth or throat. The long-term survival prospects for these turtles are not known.

A final concern is discarded **bycatch** (non target species caught incidental to normal fishing operations) which appeals to some sea turtles and causes them to concentrate in the vicinity of large scale fishing efforts where they, in turn, have a higher probability of becoming entangled in commercial gear.

© J. J. Richardsont

© National Marine Fisheries Service, NOAA

© Scott A. Eckert

Sea turtles continue to be caught as bycatch in a variety of commercial fisheries worldwide, the modification of gear (see page 92) and technique is decreasing this impact in many (but not all) regions.

How Fishing Efforts Can Have Ecological Effects on Sea Turtles

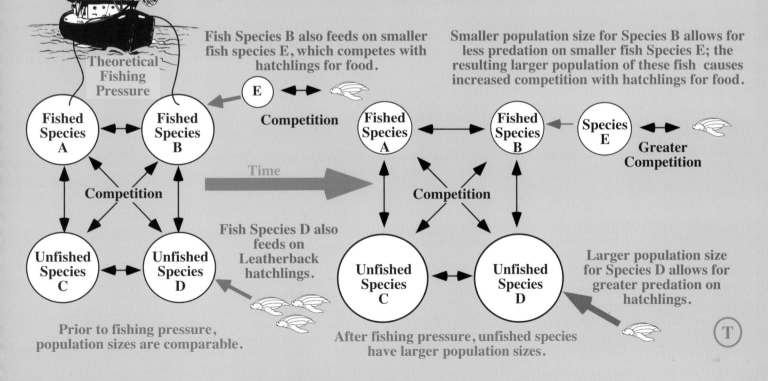

Theoretical Fishing Pressure

Fish Species B also feeds on smaller fish species E, which competes with hatchlings for food.

Smaller population size for Species B allows for less predation on smaller fish Species E; the resulting larger population of these fish causes increased competition with hatchlings for food.

E ⟷

Competition

Fished Species A ⟷ Fished Species B

Competition

Unfished Species C ⟷ Unfished Species D

Fish Species D also feeds on Leatherback hatchlings.

Time

Fished Species A ⟷ Fished Species B ← Species E ⟷

Greater Competition

Competition

Unfished Species C ⟷ Unfished Species D

Larger population size for Species D allows for greater predation on hatchlings.

Prior to fishing pressure, population sizes are comparable.

After fishing pressure, unfished species have larger population sizes.

Ⓣ

Coastal Fishing

Baitfish

The horseshoe crab, a rather strange looking animal that is actually more closely related to a land spider than it is to any crab, is one of the primary dietary items of the logger-head sea turtle. In the last decade, horseshoe crabs have undergone large population declines. This is due in part to loss of habitat, but over-fishing has also been implicated. Horseshoe crabs are used as bait by commercial fishers for conch and American eels, as well as collected for research and the production of biomedical compounds. The end result is that an animal that existed for 100 million years before dinosaurs walked the earth, is now severely threat-ened by man. For the loggerhead turtle, a primary food source is rapidly disappearing; this could cause an ecologi-cal cascade effect relating to prey selection, habitat use and predation pressures.

Gillnets

There are still places, such as Hawai'i, that allow commer-cial gillnetting of fish. This destructive and non-selective form of fishing has been banned in many places. Gillnets are often laid atop reef flats which function as primary sea turtle feeding areas. The incidental catch rate of turtles is directly related to the length of the net, its mesh size and soak time. Turtles entangled in such nets have a high risk of drowning. Setting an example for other states to follow, citizens of Florida banned the use of all gill nets in state waters in 1996.

Some gillnets are laid in the open ocean to catch sword-fish, mahi mahi, mackerals, sharks and billfish. These nets are similarly non-selective and are responsible for the deaths of large numbers of seabirds, marine mammals and turtles. Soaring incidental capture rates as the commercial use of gillnets increased in Chile and Peru in the 1980's are thought to have contributed to the collapse of the larg-est known leatherback breeding populations on earth, which until recently laid their eggs along the Pacific Mexi-can coast.

Gillnets

Hooks

Xray of green sea turtle showing hook, line and leaders inside throat.

Dead turtle caught in gill net

Shoreline

Concerns exist in Hawai'i and certain other Pacific islands regarding the effects of shoreline fishing through use of rod and reel on incidental take of sea turtles. Dis-carded fishing line (and hooks) cause additional injury and death. As with other fishing impacts, improved edu-cation of fishers could go a long way towards reducing incidental take from these activities.

Pelagic Fishing Effects

The Longline Fishery

Leatherbacks can be attracted to chemical light sticks used on the lines, perhaps confusing them for jellyfish luminescence.

Leatherbacks may become caught in float lines where their prey, sea jellies, also entangle.

Green turtles, loggerheads, and olive ridleys occasionally eat the bait and become hooked.

Subsequent mortality is usually higher for hooked turtles than for entangled ones.

Longlines are used for the capture of open ocean fish species such as tuna, swordfish, and other billfish. This is accomplished through deployment of buoyed surface lines, often several miles long, from which many smaller diameter lines are suspended down into the water column. It is from these lines that large numbers of baited hooks are attached and allowed to "soak", usually overnight. Uncounted thousands of "non-target" species (including sea turtles) are hooked every year and may die as a result. Moreover, a percentage of turtles released alive, after having been hooked, retain hooks in their digestive systems and these, too, can cause severe injury and even death over time.

Recent court action has brought this concern to the forefront. In Hawai'i, the longline fishery expanded at an amazing rate during the late 1980's; in 2000 a U. S. federal court decision effectively shut down the swordfish fishery surrounding this central Pacific archipelago due to perceived impact on critically endangered leatherback turtles.

In the Mediterranean Sea, where sea turtle bycatch is a serious conservation issue and the use of surface longlines is a time-honored tradition (apparently dating to 177 BC in Sicily), reducing fishing effort (for example, by time and area closures, limited entry fisheries, or the designation of marine reserves) is considered the most practical way to counter the various deleterious effects of commercial longlines, trawls and gill nets.

Some longlines are purposely set on the floor of coastal waters to catch bottomfish such as snapper and grouper. Such lines have the potential to entangle and hook bottom feeding sea turtles.

Shrimp Trawling and Turtle Excluder Devices (TEDs)

The development of devices that would allow turtles to escape from trawl nets began in earnest in 1978. Prior to the development of the Turtle Excluder Device (TED), tens of thousands of sea turtles drowned in shrimp trawls in U.S. waters each year. Remember, sea turtles are not fish – they must surface to breathe or they will die. Until recently, trawl-related drownings were the single largest source of sea turtle mortality in the U.S. The use of TEDs has allowed for continued fishing while decreasing the number of sea turtles caught by as much as 97%. A variety of approved designs provide for the necessary escape mechanism, at a cost between $50 - $400 per unit. A reduction in the bycatch volume of non-target finfish is achieved through the use of a secondary device called a BRD (bycatch reduction device). Such devices can reduce fish bycatch from 29% to 49%.

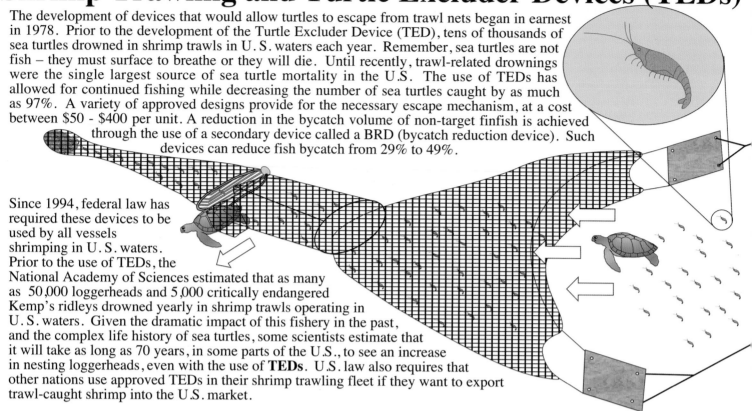

Since 1994, federal law has required these devices to be used by all vessels shrimping in U.S. waters. Prior to the use of TEDs, the National Academy of Sciences estimated that as many as 50,000 loggerheads and 5,000 critically endangered Kemp's ridleys drowned yearly in shrimp trawls operating in U.S. waters. Given the dramatic impact of this fishery in the past, and the complex life history of sea turtles, some scientists estimate that it will take as long as 70 years, in some parts of the U.S., to see an increase in nesting loggerheads, even with the use of **TEDs**. U.S. law also requires that other nations use approved TEDs in their shrimp trawling fleet if they want to export trawl-caught shrimp into the U.S. market.

Other Measures

Seasonal closures and area restrictions, along with reductions in the net-towing time for each shrimping run, have also contributed to a decrease in incidental turtle captures. We know this because the U.S. National Marine Fisheries Service maintains a nation-wide network of volunteers that monitor the coastlines and report when dead turtles wash ashore.

How It Works:

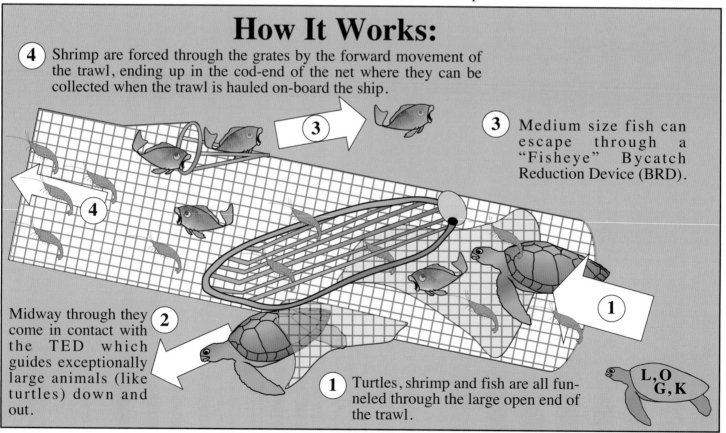

4 Shrimp are forced through the grates by the forward movement of the trawl, ending up in the cod-end of the net where they can be collected when the trawl is hauled on-board the ship.

3 Medium size fish can escape through a "Fisheye" Bycatch Reduction Device (BRD).

2 Midway through they come in contact with the TED which guides exceptionally large animals (like turtles) down and out.

1 Turtles, shrimp and fish are all funneled through the large open end of the trawl.

L, O, G, K

Modified after NOAA/NMFS 2002

Introduced Species

Introduction of non-indigenous coastal plants, especially fast-growing varieties, may reduce the suitability of beaches for nesting by eliminating native vegetation, overgrowing sandy areas, and contributing to egg mortality through root invasion of nest cavities.

Alien plants, such as ironwood trees (*Casuarina equisetifolia*), can create impenetrable barriers to egg-laden females trying to dig a nest. Marine alien species are also a major concern; introduced species such as *Kapaphycus striatum* can overgrow and dominate nearshore areas in Hawai‘i, completely altering important feeding and resting habitats. Such alien algae can overgrow and displace native seaweeds or seagrasses that make-up the diet of green sea turtles. Similarly, overgrowth of native seaweeds, seagrasses, and, in some cases, living coral reef can result in loss of habitat necessary to support sea turtles and/or their prey populations.

© Jen Smith

Kappaphycus alverezii, an alien seaweed, overgrowing and killing-off the native, reef-building coral *Porites compressa* in Kane‘ohe Bay, Hawai‘i. Such a habitat shift can dramatically affect sea turtle populations that use such habitat for feeding and resting.

G H

Alien ironwood trees (*Cassurina* sp.) form an impenetrable barrier to any female turtle coming ashore to nest. Their salt-tolerant roots extend deep into the sand and prove to be a rock-hard wall against the flippers of any turtle trying to dig a nest in the sand.

Alien species may also introduce diseases and parasites that can spread through an environment and negatively affect sea turtles and/or their prey.

Interestingly, turtles themselves may serve to move plants and organisms thousands of miles, perhaps serving as a mechanism of introduction themselves!

National Marine Sanctuary Program, NOAA

Alien seaweeds are causing complete phase shifts on Hawaiian coral reefs, changing them from diverse live coral habitat with many species of native algae for green sea turtles to forage on, to monospecific deserts, devoid of live coral and many coral reef-associated species.

On the island of Maui, another alien seaweed has displaced the native food source for this turtle.

© Ursula Keuper-Bennett/Peter Bennett

© Jen Smith

Green sea turtle sleeping hole atop coral reef now filled with alien seaweed

With nowhere to sleep, and their traditional food sources overgrown by aliens, where's a turtle to go?

© Jen Smith

© Jen Smith

Marine Debris

Marine debris poses hazards both through ingestion and entanglement. Ingested marine debris may cause choking, starvation or be toxic; it's estimated that somewhere between one third to one half of all sea turtles ingest plastic products. Juvenile turtles of most species appear to be especially vulnerable to debris ingestion.

© Kendra Choquette-D'Avella

Marine debris washed ashore can deter a female from crawling up a beach to nest, can prevent basking behavior, or can inhibit a hatchling from reaching the ocean.

© Chris Johnson, Marinelife Center of Juno Beach

To many turtles, discarded plastic (trash bags, rings, bottles, wrap, etc.), styrofoam, packaging materials, and latex balloons may resemble sea jellies. Aluminum foil, fish hooks and mylar can resemble small surface fish. Sharp plastics, glass and metals, once ingested, can cut stomachs and intestines, causing internal infections. Swallowing of these non-digestible items can cause stomach and intestinal blockage, while at the same time making the animal think it's full so that it slowly starves to death or is too weakened to survive. Non-fatal ingestion of marine debris can also introduce toxins into sea turtles.

ALERT: The dumping of plastic-bagged garbage at sea, even in small amounts, can result in the bag being ingested by sea turtles.

© Scott A. Eckert

Effects of Marine Debris on Sea Turtles

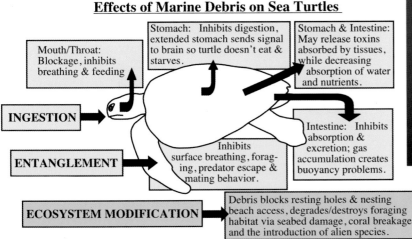

Mouth/Throat: Blockage, inhibits breathing & feeding

Stomach: Inhibits digestion, extended stomach sends signal to brain so turtle doesn't eat & starves.

Stomach & Intestine: May release toxins absorbed by tissues, while decreasing absorption of water and nutrients.

INGESTION

ENTANGLEMENT

Inhibits surface breathing, foraging, predator escape & mating behavior.

Intestine: Inhibits absorption & excretion; gas accumulation creates buoyancy problems.

ECOSYSTEM MODIFICATION

Debris blocks resting holes & nesting beach access, degrades/destroys foraging habitat via seabed damage, coral breakage, and the introduction of alien species.

Other debris in the water may inhibit feeding or mating activities. Entanglement in large masses of marine debris can lead to starvation, drowning, and an increased vulnerability to predators or boat collisions.

Pollution

Other Contaminants

Heavy metals and PCBs are known to cause a range of health problems and sometimes death in fish and invertebrates. Direct impact on sea turtles has not been well studied, but a recent investigation in Australia has shown that certain metals tend to concentrate in the liver and kidneys. Cadmium, a trace metal, actually concentrates within edible tissues in a number of species of sea turtles. Other concerns exist regarding loss of physiological function, displacement of prey items, or degradation of necessary habitat due to pollution.

Bloom of *Cladophora* seaweed off the island of Maui.

© Ursula Keuper-Bennett/Peter Bennett

Oil Spills

As crude oil floats on the surface of the ocean, it starts to degrade into what we recognize as tar balls. Floating tar balls may be fed upon by juvenile, sub-adult and adult turtles, reducing the ability of these animals to further feed; ingestion of oil-based substances can also cause severe organ damage. Oil can clog the animal's nostrils and cover the shell with tar, causing drag and impeding survival. As petroleum products wash ashore they can degrade prime nesting habitat, inhibit nesting behavior by adult females, soak into nest cavities, and/or prevent hatchlings from reaching the ocean.

© Ursula Keuper-Bennett/Peter Bennett

Nutrients

Excessive nutrient loads in nearshore environments can often cause extensive algal blooms, clogging the water column, over-growing prey habitat, reducing prey abundance, clogging resting holes and cleaning stations, and serving as substrates for bacteria and diseases. The decrease in water quality that accompanies algal blooms affects organisms throughout the ecosystem and can cause cascade effects, which may result in sea turtles leaving an area. Often such blooms are caused by non-point source nutrient inputs to the ocean, originating with fertilizers used for agriculture and gardens or the ineffective treatment of human sewage.

Oil Spills

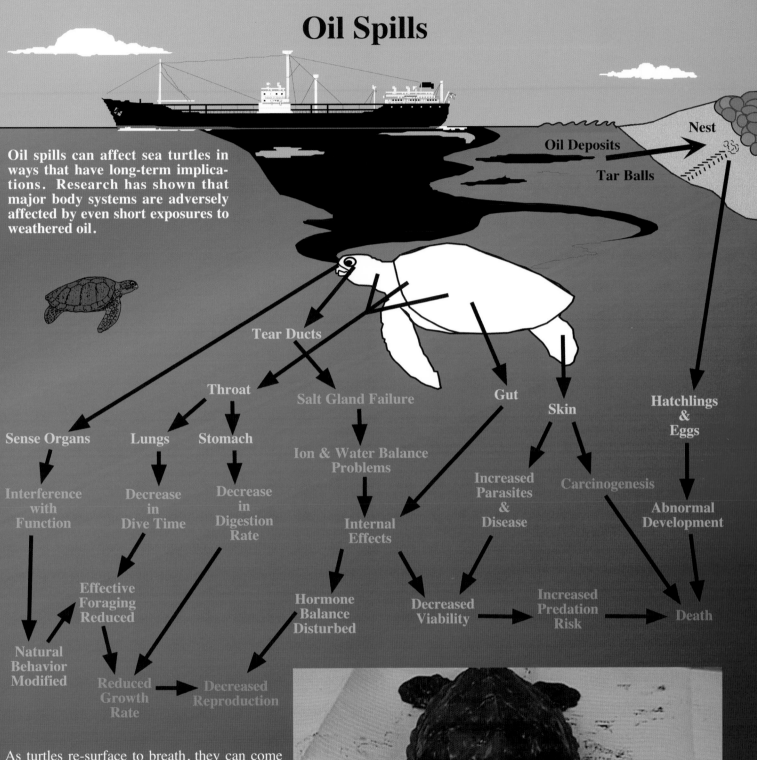

Oil spills can affect sea turtles in ways that have long-term implications. Research has shown that major body systems are adversely affected by even short exposures to weathered oil.

Nest

Oil Deposits

Tar Balls

Tear Ducts

Throat

Salt Gland Failure

Gut

Skin

Hatchlings & Eggs

Sense Organs

Lungs

Stomach

Ion & Water Balance Problems

Increased Parasites & Disease

Carcinogenesis

Interference with Function

Decrease in Dive Time

Decrease in Digestion Rate

Internal Effects

Abnormal Development

Effective Foraging Reduced

Hormone Balance Disturbed

Decreased Viability

Increased Predation Risk

Death

Natural Behavior Modified

Reduced Growth Rate

Decreased Reproduction

As turtles re-surface to breath, they can come in contact with surface spills. Oiled turtles often require specialized cleaning by an oil spill emergency response team. As for the poor little oiled turtle on the right, he was cleaned (with Kraft® mayonnaise!) and released back into the wild; wow, learn something new every day...

Harvesting Sea Turtles

ALERT: IT IS AGAINST INTERNATIONAL LAW TO CARRY SEA TURTLE PARTS OR PRODUCTS ACROSS NATIONAL BORDERS. IN THE UNITED STATES AND MANY OTHER COUNTRIES, IT IS ILLEGAL TO SELL, PURCHASE OR POSSESS SEA TURTLES OR ANY PRODUCTS DERIVED FROM THEM.

© David Schrichte

Sea turtle eggs have been (and in many cases still are) used for food by people all over the world. Some cultures believe that eating eggs promotes long life, as turtles are amongst the longest living animals on the planet. Others view eating turtle eggs as an **aphrodisiac**; purportedly due to the lengthy time that

© Scott A. Eckert

sea turtles spend copulating. Like so many proclaimed sexual or life-lengthening aids made from animal products, there is no scientific evidence to support these claims. In terms of protein and energy, a chicken egg is more nutritious than the egg of a leatherback turtle.

There are still indigenous peoples that hunt sea turtles or gather their eggs for food. In general, however, the historical subsistence hunting of sea turtles cannot be compared with the modern era commercial take of turtles, and it is primarily the latter that is implicated in the most dramatic sea turtle population declines worldwide. As traditional subsistence hunting, particularly in island-based cultures, is increasingly replaced by currency-based economies, the distinction between commercial and cultural take may become blurred. As turtle populations decline and hunters continue to target nesting females, the trend is exasperated by eliminating not only the female but the many thousands of eggs she would have laid ... and all of the future generations she was capable of producing.

© David Schrichte

Many governments prohibit take of sea turtles at all times or during certain times of the year, but effective enforcement is rare. Moreover, many countries' sea turtle "conservation" laws set minimum size limits that protect juveniles but leave breeding age adults legally vulnerable to harvest. In late-maturing, long-lived species such as sea turtles, this type of management strategy is a recipe for disaster.

© Scott A. Eckert

© Scott A. Eckert

Traditional "women's money" from Palau made from hawksbill's shell scutes.

Leatherback oil used for a wide variety of purposes, from varnishing boats to medicinal uses.

The Big Picture: Products from Sea Turtles

	Flatback Sea Turtle	Green Sea Turtle	Hawksbill Sea Turtle	Olive Ridley Sea Turtle	Kemp's Ridley Sea Turtle	Loggerhead Sea Turtle	Leatherback Sea Turtle
Bone — Bone meal							
Carapace — Curio, lacquered wall hangings, baby cradles							
Tortoiseshell, Carey			5				
Eggs — Food, aphrodisiac associations in some cultures						8	
Fatty Tissue — Used to make oil, cream							10
Meat — Staple food item for some cultures, ceremonial or gourmet item for others		1	6				11
Shell		2				9	
Skin — Tanned and used as leather for producing purses, shoes & clothing		3		7			
Soup — Made from both the meat and the fatty tissue (calipee)		4					
Whole Animal — Stuffed and sold as curios							

© David Schrichte

Question: Why don't we captive-rear endangered sea turtles in order to provide these products? Wouldn't that decrease the take of wild specimens? Reasonable people disagree on this point. Some argue that by promoting public demand for endangered species products, especially from species in relatively poor countries where smuggling is lucrative and impossible to control, a black market rages, fueled by a demand for luxury products (jewelry, cosmetic creams, leather) in wealthier countries. In the end, more specimens are taken from the wild than before. Moreover, in some cases wild specimens are continually harvested for breeding purposes, and biologists express concern about genetic mixing, diseases moving from aquaculture facilities into wild populations, and other issues. Proponents counter that captive rearing can supply products predictably and profitably, earning income for conservation and reducing pressures on wild stocks. What do you think?

1. Historically a reliable source of fresh meat for transoceanic sailors.

2. Used traditionally as housing material by tribes in Mexico.

3. Skin used as footwear by traditional tribes in Mexico.

4. The green turtle is commonly known as the "soup turtle".

5. Scutes (=colorful shell plates) - Used to produce various forms of jewelry, hairbrushes. combs & curios. In Japan the art is centuries old and well-developed culturally. In Palau (Western Pacific), the shell is used by husbands to make "women's money" or *toluk* for their wives.

6. Reported to cause fatal illness in rare cases throughout the world.

7. Raw material for leather products; export to Japan was the most important reason for the dramatic decline in many eastern Pacific populations of olive ridleys during the last quarter of the 20th century.

8. Historically in some parts of the world, the eggs were dried in the oviduct and sold like sausage.

9. Traditionally used in Honduras to make paddle boats.

10. Used historically to produce oil for lamps & stoves, varnishing boats, cosmetics, and, when taken internally, for medicinal, aphrodisiac, or life-prolonging effects.

11. Food item in some cultures; usually dried or stewed (the least-favored among sea turtle meats).

Tourism

© Jeff Kuwabara

While sea turtles pose little risk to swimmers, snorkelers or divers, sadly the reverse is not necessarily true. Harassment (including attempts to catch or ride a sleeping or foraging turtle) can seriously stress the animal and discourage it from visiting what may be prime resting or feeding habitat. Any form of harassment is illegal in the U.S. and in some other countries, as well.

Ill-planned coastal development and careless recreational practices can cause severe degradation of nesting grounds, affect sex determination (for example, by removing native vegetation and changing beach temperature) which can alter sex ratios for an adult population far into the future, displace turtles into marginal habitats, and even result in beach loss by increasing erosion.

© Scott A. Eckert

© David Schrichte

↑ The proliferation of all-terrain vehicles in close proximity to nesting beaches is a recipe for disaster, as seen with this disrupted nest on an isolated beach in Baja, California, Mexico.

High density beach-related tourism can have devastating effects on coastal areas where sea turtles nest. Sometimes the effects can be reduced through education to modify the behavior of both the tourists and the industry that serves them. Examples include the need to discourage feeding of feral animals, as well as to encourage the placement of buildings and roadways (which bring lighting and increased activity) a safe distance away from nesting beaches.

The Effects of Divers

Surprisingly, divers and snorkelors are not reported to be having the direct impact on sea turtles that one might think, given the increasing popularity of SCUBA diving and the close proximity of divers to sea turtles in many areas. There are concerns related to imprinting, which can result when turtles are hand-fed and may cause changes in natural behaviors, and related to the interruption of natural feeding, basking, resting, nesting or mating cycles that may cause animals to retreat to marginal habitats where food is scarce, predators more abundant, nest success reduced, etc. An increasing concern relates to overuse by commercial tour operators of certain areas where turtles are prevalent. By placing large numbers of divers and snorkelors in the water with these animals seven days a week, fifty-two weeks a year, the ecosystem itself can be irreparably degraded.

Many areas and commercial operators are starting to take steps to regulate diver and snorkelor activities to prevent overuse, and the subsequent loss of the proverbial "goose that laid the golden egg". Educating tourists as to proper behavior, maintaining appropriate distances, and preventing too many people from being in the water near these animals at one time, are all steps in the right direction. Partnerships between resource management agencies and tour industry groups can lead to a win-win situation for all involved. The Wider Caribbean Sea Turtle Conservation Network (WIDECAST) and other groups are actively involved in promoting sustainable practices (see page 111).

Kendra Choquette-D'Avella

Kendra Choquette-D'Avella

Kendra Choquette-D'Avella

The snorkeler (*above*) and divers (*left*) are maintaining enough distance between themselves and the turtles so as not to effect natural patterns of behavior. The animal is not "penned-in" by the divers' activities, and their slow movements through the water do not alarm the animals.

CONSERVATION

"Wildlife management and biological conservation are as much about managing people as managing wildlife: in the end, they are politics - not biology. Marine turtles have persisted for eons, prospering without protected areas, conservation laws, action plans, research manuals, and other accouterments of conservation programs. It is when people are involved, with over-exploitation and habitat perturbation, that biological conservation becomes essential."

J. G. Frazier (1999), Smithsonian Institution

© Scott A. Eckert

There is growing awareness that reptiles worldwide are under increasing environmental and human-induced stresses. Currently, the U. S. Endangered Species Act lists 26 species of amphibians and 88 species of reptiles as Threatened or Endangered. At a greater scale, the World Conservation Union classifies 129 amphibians and 270 reptiles worldwide as Vulnerable, Endangered or Critically Endangered. Worldwide, reptiles are faced with markets for their meat and eggs, as well as for their parts and products (leather, oil and creams, shell crafts, stuffed curios). Turtles are sacrificed for cultural rituals (symbolizing long life, for example) and, along with many species of lizards and snakes, illegally collected by the millions for the pet trade. Snakes and crocodiles are wantonly destroyed in many areas for the real or perceived threat they pose to humans. Habitat destruction, pollution, unintentional mortality (fisheries bycatch, road kills, the pet trade), and the introduction of exotic species have also contributed to widespread population declines.

Conservation is a broadly encompassing science. "Conservation" is defined by the IUCN World Conservation Strategy as "...the management of human use of organisms or ecosystems to ensure such use is sustainable. Besides sustainable use, conservation includes protection, maintenance, rehabilitation, restoration, and enhancement of populations and ecosystems." We hope that through reading this book, you have gained a greater appreciation for the complexities of conservation by learning more about the intricacies of sea turtle ecology, including the linkages that define a sea turtle's **niche**, the effects that human development and cultural norms have had on sea turtle survival, and the many different types of habitats needed to support healthy sea turtle populations.

When a sea turtle population is identified as threatened and in need of "conservation," what is really meant? Designating a population (or species) as threatened or endangered implies that we are unwilling to stand by and watch it disappear. A judgment has been made, and a course of action is required. Where to start? Because not every threat can be reduced or eliminated, managers prioritize threats in order to advocate for the allocation of staff, funding, and other limited resources. Dealing effectively with priority threats may require changes in the legislative framework, the designation of parks or protected areas, the invention of new technologies. Ongoing monitoring of depleted populations enables a manager to evaluate the success of such measures.

© Robert Thorn

© David Schrichte

There are no simple answers to the unprecedented loss of species that our planet is currently experiencing. But there are some things we know. We know that effective conservation must be holistic, integrated, solution-oriented, and people-friendly. And we know that fragmenting large areas into pockets of small refuges surrounded by human development is unlikely to produce a lasting benefit, nor is the trading of natural environments for artificial ones necessarily a good thing. For in so doing the very fabric of earth's sustaining **ecosystems** is torn, replaced by tattered fragments-- isolated habitats with little, if any, connectivity in terms of basic ecological services.

Often there are differing opinions concerning which conservation measures are likely to be most successful. Some may argue that protecting nesting beaches is a priority. Others counter that too much natural nesting habitat has already been lost, and greater effort should be made to encourage reproduction in zoos or commercial farms. And what of protecting foraging habitat? Mandating responsible coastal development? Providing incentives for responsible fishing? Encouraging collaboration among neighboring governments? Educating tourists? Engaging local communities in meaningful dialogue on alternate livelihoods? These, too, would seem to be essential ingredients for success.

© Scott A. Eckert

Management Efforts

In the U. S., federal management of sea turtles falls to the National Marine Fisheries Service, which is responsible for protecting and managing sea turtles in the marine environment, and the Fish and Wildlife Service, which has primary jurisdiction over sea turtles onshore. To fulfill their management mandate the federal agencies work collaboratively with state governments, as well as with nongovernmental organizations at the community level that encourage a sense of stewardship over local nesting and feeding areas. Management authorities at all levels depend on each of us to pay attention to the rules and regulations protecting endangered species and their habitats.

©Scott A. Eckert

The centerpiece of sea turtle management in the U. S. is the fact that sea turtles are completely protected by federal law. This premise sets the stage for actions that range from lighting ordinances along the coast of Florida to suspension of commercial longline fishing in the Central Pacific. The U. S. is not alone in protecting its sea turtles, a number of other countries have similar laws in place.

Perhaps the biggest challenge to management is this, "How do we define success?" Are we hoping simply to prevent extinction? Or are we trying to return populations to historical levels, assuming we know what those levels were? Maybe our goal is to have just enough turtles so that a catastrophe, such as a major oil spill, doesn't wipe them all out. Or to maintain populations sufficiently large that they can sustain a profitable commercial harvest. Federal management agencies are tasked with developing recovery plans for endangered species that define recovery goals and criteria and an implementation schedule for priority actions, thereby helping to ensure that "management" has a game plan.

Bottom line: "Management" is where sea turtles and people meet. It takes creative genius at times to forge a strategy that humans can accept and sea turtles can live with –literally.

Some of the most successful management initiatives create opportunities for those closest to the resource to participate meaningfully and even profitably in conservation measures. At certain sites in Costa Rica, for example, local villagers are allowed to collect and sell a percentage of olive ridley eggs laid during **arribada**-style nesting. In exchange, villagers leave the remaining eggs undisturbed and help to protect them from predators and poachers. As a result, the village has an economic incentive for conserving the turtles and a higher percentage of the eggs hatch than would otherwise be the case. In the absence of the controlled harvest, females nesting later in the season exhume eggs laid earlier, reducing hatch success all around.

© Dave Gulko

ATTENTION BEACH USERS

HELP PROTECT ENDANGERED SEA TURTLES
·AVOID DISTURBING NESTING FEMALES
·LEAVE NEST, EGGS AND HATCHLINGS UNDISTURBED
·TURN OFF LIGHTS THAT SHINE ON BEACH
(BETWEEN MAY 1ST OCT. 31ST)
SEA TURTLES ARE PROTECTED BY COUNTY STATE
AND FEDERAL LAW. FINES UP TO $20,000.
FOR MORE INFO. CONTACT 633-2016

NO GLASS CONTAINERS ON BEACH
$500. FINE OR 60 DAYS
CITY CODE 5.57

NO ANIMALS ON BEACH OR IN PARKS
$100. FINE OR 30 DAYS
CITY CODE 4.15

NO LITTERING
$500. FINE OR 60 DAYS
FLA STATUE 403

NO OPEN ALCOHOL CONTAINERS
ON CROSSOVERS
$500. FINE AND 60 DAYS
CITY CODE 15 - 20.1

+ ENFORCED +

© David Schrichte

How Do We Obtain Data on Sea Turtles Over Time

The successful management of sea turtles relies heavily on being able to answer natural history questions about nesting migrations, the pelagic-stage "lost years", coastal home ranges, residency times, feeding habits, etc. This often requires surveillance of individuals without affecting natural behaviors, and can be accomplished through the use of one or more of the following techniques:

- Remote Sensing Technology (Satellite or VHF Telemetry)

- Passive Tags (external, internal)

- Genetic Markers

Satellite Telemetry

Advances in microtechnology have allowed researchers to make use of transmitters and satellites to track the movements of turtles across oceans. Information regarding location, depth and duration of recent dives, and environmental indicators (such as water temperature) can all be easily logged and transmitted. These data provide unique insight into migration and navigation, mating and foraging, and even the potential for interaction with high seas fishing fleets.

Instruments attached to a turtle must not interfere with the behavior or health of the animal. Issues such as weight, durability and hydrodynamics need to be considered in designing such units.

② A passing satellite receives the signal and re-transmits the data to a ground station.

① The turtle is fitted with a satellite transmitter, which sends a signal to an orbiting satellite.

③ A researcher who just a couple years ago might face bouts of seasickness on a boat for days following the animal around, can now sit in his (or her) office and receive location and behavioral data simultaneously from transmitter-equipped animals widely dispersed around the world.

Passive Tags

Conservation and management programs are deemed successful if the target population of sea turtles recovers to the point that it is no longer considered threatened or endangered. One of the most useful tools that managers can employ in evaluating the status of a sea turtle population is a passive tag. Tags allow scientists to identify individual turtles, and to use information compiled over time to determine nesting periodicity, population trends, growth rates, survival rates, and other important information.

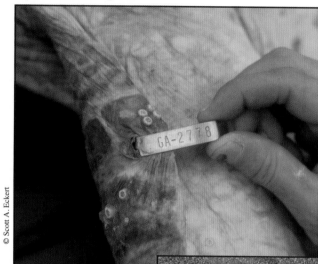

© Scott A. Eckert

National Marine Fisheries Service, NOAA

The most commonly used passive tags are external flipper tags. Flipper tags are placed on the trailing edge of the forelimbs and/or hind limbs; the process of attaching a flipper tag is analogous to piercing an earlobe and does not cause lasting harm or alter the animal's behavior. Two types of external tags are commonly used: plastic and metal. A unique code consisting of numbers and letters is stamped on the surface of the tag. There are various problems with the use of external tags, including tag corrosion and loss, fouling, and, according to one study, increased likelihood of the tag (and its turtle) becoming entangled in a gill net.

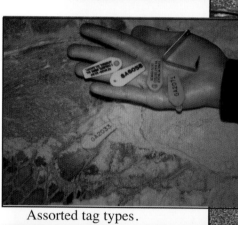

© Scott A. Eckert

Assorted tag types.

© Chris Johnson, Marinelife Center of Juno Beach

Note: If you see a tagged turtle, record both the number and (on the reverse side) the return address on the tag. Present this information to the local fisheries authority. **Never** remove a tag from a live turtle, and never harass a turtle in order to read a tag number.

© Kendra Choquette-D'Avella

© Kendra Choquette-D'Avella

"Living tags" offer the ability to tag a young juvenile and have the tag remain with the animal through its life without the concerns regarding tag loss seen with plastic or metal flipper tags. With living tags, a small plug of plastron tissue is surgically implanted into the carapace; since the plastron is usually lighter in color than the carapace, the mark is easily seen over time as the animal grows and matures. This unique methodology is perhaps best known for the role it played in marking young Kemp's ridley turtles as part of the long-term binational conservation program between the U.S. and Mexico that has resulted in the establishment of a small nesting colony in Texas.

Internal tags involve the injection of small devices under the skin that can be detected by x-ray or with a hand-held reader device. Unlike external flipper tags, internal tags are rarely lost.

© Kendra Choquette-D'Avella

© David Schrichte

Interestingly, there may be a turtle form of fingerprints, er, flipperprints. Patterns formed by the flipper scales and the intervening spaces between them may be able to function for identification of individual juvenile Kemp's ridley turtles. Similarly, some scientists are able to identify individual leatherback turtles by the size and shape of an irregular-shaped pink spot on the crown of their heads.

Finally, a high tech "tag" of sorts involves advances in genetic technology that have contributed to the identification of sea turtle populations. For example, three genetically distinct subpopulations of loggerheads have been found along the southeastern coast of the U.S. Such data can be used to help determine "Critical Habitat", which in the United States allows for protection of habitat deemed absolutely necessary for the survival of a species listed under the Endangered Species Act. Critical Habitat designation is one of the most important tools available to protect prime nesting habitat and nearshore feeding areas; in doing so, such protection often has the side benefit of safeguarding important habitat for a wide variety of other species.

© David Schrichte

Olive ridley turtle caught in gill net

© Kendra Choquette-D'Avella

Legislative Tools

The U. S. Endangered Species Act (ESA): Does It Work? In Hawai'i, prior to the listing of the green sea turtle as a "Threatened" species under the ESA in 1978, green turtles were declining due primarily to excessive fishing pressure. One rarely observed these animals foraging close to shore during daylight hours. Twenty-five years (and nearly a generation) later, with the protection provided under the ESA, green turtle populations are rising and Hawai'i has the greatest nesting density of green turtles in the Central Pacific. Today green turtles feed close to shore both day and night and even bask during daylight hours on the main Hawaiian islands.

Parks and Refuges

In 1990, the U. S. Congress established the Archie Carr National Wildlife Refuge. Named after the famous sea turtle biologist and located on two barrier islands off the coast of Florida, the refuge extends approximately 20 miles and is one of the most important nesting areas, primarily for loggerhead turtles, in the world. National wildlife refuges and national marine sanctuaries are important tools in safeguarding critical habitat and minimizing human impacts on important turtle behaviors such as nesting, mating and feeding.

© Scott A. Eckert

Nesting and Nest Protection Efforts

Legislation gives natural resource management agencies the authority to issue permits to organizations and trained individuals who actively participate in conservation efforts, such as removing eggs from high risk zones and relocating them to higher ground or to protected hatcheries. Other successful strategies involve obscuring nesting crawls, keeping nest sites under surveillance, and regularly patrolling nesting beaches.

The Dawn Patrol

In many areas, the presence of law enforcement or researchers on a nesting beach can reduce dramatically a wide range of threats to sea turtles and their young. In many areas it's difficult to position such people full-time during the nesting season...still, the need for beach patrols to minimize poaching, predation, and human activity in close proximity to the nests calls for some sort of presence. Enter organized volunteer groups. Every year, around the globe, intrepid groups of volunteers monitor beaches, looking for turtle tracks and helping to protect eggs and hatchlings. Combining the efforts of a country's management agencies, NGOs and often a very strong local community, these cooperative volunteer-based efforts are assisting in the recovery of turtles by protecting them at their most vulnerable times and places.

© Scott A. Eckert

Involving The Public

The Role of Zoos & Aquariums

Zoos and aquariums have broad mandates that embrace public education and recreation, as well as conservation and science. Those that display sea turtles allow the public the unique experience of learning about these animals first hand. Many of the turtles on display were either born in captivity or previously underwent some sort of trauma that prevented them from returning to the wild.

Such institutions also offer a relatively safe and stable environment for scientists to study the physiology and behavior of captive animals. These institutions also tend to have the expertise and facilities to assist in treatment and recovery of injured turtles, and the expertise amongst their staff to assist managers in dealing with wildlife issues in the field.

Ecotourism ("Turtle Watching")

Changing the way the average person views his or her relationship with nature will go a long way towards making conservation practices more successful.

Customs and enforcement officials continue to confiscate jewelry and curios brought in by careless or uniformed travelers.

For countries with sufficient numbers of sea turtles surviving within their borders, the shift from harvesting turtles to "sea turtle ecotourism" can be very lucrative, especially at the community level. Moreover, the opportunity to bring tourists and turtles together under mutually beneficial circumstances has the potential to significantly enhance sea turtle survival.

Ill-conceived ecotourism programs, however, do more harm than good. These may include riding turtles, excessive lights and noise, and the retaining of hatchlings for days at a time until large numbers of them are available for tourists to release to the sea (usually for a fee). Excessive handling of hatchlings and the holding of these animals for display can cause stress, the expenditure of limited energy resources (which the hatchling will need for a successful "swim frenzy" to the open ocean), and increased predation due to day releases.

Visualizing the Future

By now it should be clear that whether or not sea turtles survive ultimately depends on what actions ordinary people are willing to take ... and how effectively that action can be coordinated among communities and nations. Sea turtles are migratory throughout their long lives, meaning that a shared conservation vision has to be articulated at the scale of ocean basins, not simply at the level of individual nesting beaches or feeding grounds.

The Wider Caribbean Sea Turtle Conservation Network (WIDECAST) was founded more than two decades ago to accomplish just such an objective. With experts serving as volunteer Country Coordinators in nearly 40 nations and territories, WIDECAST focuses on bringing the best available science to bear on sea turtle management and conservation, empowering stakeholders to make effective use of that science in the policy-making process, and providing a mechanism and a framework for cooperation at all levels, both within and among the nations of the Caribbean Sea.

By emphasizing information exchange and training, the network focuses on initiatives that build leadership capacity within participating countries and institutions. And by working closely with local communities and resource managers, standard management guidelines have been developed that promote best practices and sustainability, ensuring that current utilization practices, whether consumptive (as in harvest) or non-consumptive (as in ecotourism), do not undermine sea turtle survival over the long term.

By joining together to protect future options with regard to the use of sea turtles, network participants recognize essential linkages between a healthy Caribbean ecosystem and economic prosperity for Caribbean people. Integrated programs such as this one offer hope for the future!

WWW.WIDECAST.ORG

"We see WIDECAST as a model initiative. By defining conservation priorities based on sound science, promoting consensus and emphasizing public awareness, the network has successfully integrated once isolated efforts into a collaborative regional response to the shared challenge of depleted sea turtle populations in our region."
- Alessandra Vanzella-Khouri
UNEP Caribbean Environment Programme

Visualizing the Future:

WIDECAST

and the Conservation of Caribbean Sea Turtles

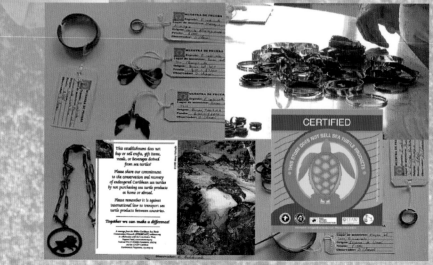

TURTLE WATCHING

Sea turtles have lived in the world's oceans for more than 150 million years. Sadly these ancient reptiles are now globally threatened with extinction. Many populations are declining as a result of persistent hunting, increasing coastal development, incidental capture in fisheries, the degradation and destruction of nesting beaches, and marine pollution. You can help to protect them by following these simple guidelines.

Developed in collaboration with the Wider Caribbean Sea Turtle Conservation Network (WIDECAST), these guidelines are intended to give general advice only – be sure to find out about local rules and regulations.

TURTLE FACTS

- All species of sea turtle are endangered and need our protection
- Turtles breathe air just like us, which means they can drown if they are prevented from reaching the surface of the sea
- Litter is dangerous, especially plastic bags which can be mistaken for jellyfish – a favourite turtle food
- Turtles remain in the same area for years and, as adults, return to the same nesting area year after year – if a nesting colony is destroyed, the turtles may never return

WHAT YOU CAN DO

- Support local sea turtle conservation initiatives – consider volunteering!
- Participate in local sighting networks and complete all sighting forms
- Do not buy or sell sea turtle products – turtles are strictly protected under CITES (Convention on International Trade in Endangered Species of Wild Fauna and Flora) and most national laws

ON THE WATER

- Keep a good look out for sea turtles while boating – boat strikes can kill
- When in the water, keep your distance and avoid startling turtles; avoid disturbing resting, sleeping or actively feeding turtles
- To ensure that encounters are as unthreatening as possible, approach turtles slowly and calmly and move away if the turtle shows signs of distress
- Never try to spear, harass, catch or ride turtles
- Experts advise not to touch or feed wild turtles
- Take all litter home with you: trash can kill, especially when it is mistaken for food

Participating in turtle watching programmes actually helps to protect turtles by raising awareness about them

Be sure to find out about local laws and regulations, as they may differ from these general guidelines

TURTLE WATCHING

ON THE BEACH

During breeding seasons, some special considerations apply to turtle nesting beaches.

- Avoid damage to incubating nests – for example, avoid driving on a turtle nesting beach or using these beaches for camp fires or barbecues
- Do not leave large items (such as chairs, umbrellas or recreational vehicles) on nesting beaches at night – these can obstruct a turtle's path and prevent egg-laying
- Keep pets, especially dogs, away as they can endanger eggs and hatchlings
- Keep beach lighting to a minimum – artificial lighting disorients turtles
- Shield or switch off lighting which is visible from the beach

Watching nesting turtles

Seeing an adult turtle come on shore to lay her eggs is an unforgettable experience. However, on land turtles are very vulnerable and if startled, a female turtle may return to the sea before her eggs can be successfully laid. Please follow these simple rules when watching nesting turtles.

- Keep disturbance to a minimum – stay quiet and move around slowly
- Do not approach turtles as they arrive from the sea: they are easily frightened off
- Turtles that have not yet laid their eggs must be left alone
- Make minimal use of flashlights; never shine lights directly into a turtle's face
- Try not to "trap" turtles – approach them from behind and keep low to the ground
- Move away if the turtle shows signs of distress
- Turtle eggs and hatchlings should be left undisturbed
- Consider limiting viewing to 30 minutes at a time

Photography

Flash photography of nesting turtles is a controversial topic. In some places this constitutes harassment and is illegal. If using a camera flash, do so sparingly and:

- Never take photographs before a turtle has laid her eggs
- Only take photographs from behind the turtle – the flash will temporarily "blind" her and complicate her return to the sea

Hatchling turtles

- Try to shield hatchlings if they appear disoriented by beachfront lighting – place yourself between the hatchlings and the light source, and ask that the lights be turned off long enough for the hatchlings to reach the sea
- Do not interfere with their crawl to the sea as this could jeopardize their survival
- Never photograph hatchlings – they are very sensitive to light

The Coral Reef Alliance (CORAL) is a member-supported, non-profit international organization dedicated to keeping coral reefs alive around the world. Visit our website http://www.coral.org

Visit the Wider Caribbean Sea Turtle Conservation Network (WIDECAST) website at http://www.widecast.org for more information on marine turtles and turtle conservation

CORAL. Used with permission. Suggestions for improving these guidelines should be sent to info@coral.org.

CORAL RP-102-2002

THE END...

APPENDIX I. TREATIES RELEVANT TO THE CONSERVATION OF SEA TURTLES

A variety of international treaties and agreements encourage efforts to manage shared sea turtle populations.

The 1973 **Convention on International Trade in Endangered Species of Wild Fauna and Flora (CITES)** was established to protect endangered species from over-exploitation by means of a system of import and export permits. The Convention regulates international commerce in animals and plants whether dead or alive, and any recognizable parts or derivatives thereof. Appendix I lists endangered species (including all species of sea turtle), trade in which is tightly controlled and requires export/import permits. Why is it important to know this? Because CITES provisions make it illegal, for example, for a tourist to return home with sea turtle products purchased abroad.

The 1993 **Convention on Biological Diversity (CBD)** has as its objective the conservation, as well as the equitable and sustainable use, of biological diversity for present and future generations. It does not specifically protect sea turtles, but binds nations to develop national strategies, plans or programs for the conservation and sustainable use of biological diversity; to identify and monitor the status of components of biological diversity; and to develop and manage protected areas and other areas of importance for biodiversity.

The 1983 **Convention on the Conservation of Migratory Species of Wild Animals**, commonly referred to as the Convention on Migratory Species (or Bonn Convention). The Convention incorporates two appendices which list migratory species that would benefit from concerted conservation measures. Endangered species, listed in Appendix I, are fully protected. This includes all sea turtles, with the exception of the endemic Australian flatback sea turtle. Nations with Appendix I species are to endeavor to conserve their habitat, to counteract factors impeding their migration, and to control other factors that might endanger them. In general, Parties are obliged to prohibit the hunting, fishing, capturing, or harassing of these species.

The 1973 **International Convention for the Prevention of Pollution from Ships (Marpol Treaty)** is an important treaty for the conservation of the marine habitat necessary for the survival of sea turtles. Its objective is "to preserve the marine environment by achieving the complete elimination of international pollution by oil and other harmful substances". The Convention has five Annexes (one each for oil, chemicals in bulk, packaged chemicals, liquid sewage, and garbage) to regulate discharge and to minimize accidents.

In 1997, the United Nations General Assembly took note of the negative impacts to the living marine resources of the world's oceans and seas by large-scale pelagic drift-net fishing, unauthorized fishing in zones of national jurisdiction, and fisheries by-catch and discards. One result of this was an **International Ban on Pelagic Drift-Net Fishing**.

In addition to global agreements, regional treaties are also important to the conservation of sea turtles.

For example, the 2001 **Inter-American Convention for the Protection and Conservation of Sea Turtles** seeks "to promote the protection, conservation and recovery of sea turtle populations and of the habitats on which they depend, based on the best available scientific evidence, taking into account the environmental, socio-economic and cultural characteristics of the Parties." Under Article III, the Convention applies to coastal habitat in the Americas, as well as maritime areas for which the Parties exercise sovereignty under the UN Convention on the Law of the Sea (i.e. up to 200 miles from shore), thereby covering a significant portion of the ranges of sea turtles in the Western Hemisphere. The treaty requires Parties to protect and conserve sea turtle populations and their habitats; reduce the incidental capture, injury and mortality of sea turtles associated with commercial fisheries; prohibit the intentional take of, and domestic and international trade in, sea turtles, their eggs, parts and products; and foster international cooperation in the research and management of sea turtles. Additionally, the Convention specifically obligates Parties to require the use of Turtle Excluder Devices (TEDs) by commercial shrimp trawling fleets.

The 1986 **Convention for the Protection and Development of the Marine Environment of the Wider Caribbean Region (Cartagena Convention).** Parties are obliged to "individually or jointly, take all appropriate measures to protect and preserve rare or fragile ecosystems, as well as the habitat of depleted, threatened or endangered species, in the Convention area." In 2000, the Convention's Protocol Concerning Specially Protected Areas and Wildlife (SPAW) came into force, providing a mechanism whereby species of wild fauna and flora could be protected on a regional scale. Annex I includes species of plants exempt from all forms of destruction or disturbance. Annex II provides for total protection and recovery to listed species of animals. Specifically, Annex II listing prohibits (a) the taking, possession or killing (including, to the extent possible, the incidental taking, possession or killing) or commercial trade in such species, their eggs, parts or products, and (b) to the extent possible, the disturbance of such species, including all Caribbean sea turtles.

The 1990 **Convention for the Protection of the Natural Resources and Environment of the South Pacific Region (SPREP).** Parties shall "take all appropriate measures to protect and preserve rare or fragile ecosystems and depleted, threatened, or endangered flora and fauna as well as their habitat" and "establish protected areas, such as parks and reserves, and prohibit or regulate any activity likely to have adverse effects on the species, ecosystems or biological processes that such areas are designed to protect." A Regional Marine Turtle Conservation Program, developed under SPREP's Natural Resource Conservation Program, promotes sea turtle conservation and monitoring in the South Pacific Region.

In the Mediterranean Sea, the 1978 **Convention for the Protection of the Mediterranean Sea against Pollution (Barcelona Convention)** and its 1986 Protocol concerning Specially Protected Areas (SPA Protocol). The Convention has general provisions for the protection of the Mediterranean marine environment, and the SPA Protocol requires Parties to protect, preserve, and manage threatened and endangered species (including banning the killing, possession, commercial trade, and disturbance of these species), to establish protected areas, and to coordinate international conservation efforts.

The 1982 **Convention on the Conservation of European Wildlife and Natural Habitats (Bern Convention).** Its aims are to "conserve wild flora and fauna and their natural habitats whose conservation requires the cooperation of several States and to promote such cooperation. Particular emphasis is given to endangered and vulnerable species, including endangered and vulnerable migratory species." Five species of sea turtles (green, loggerhead, hawksbill, leatherback & Kemp's ridley) are listed in Appendix II as strictly protected species. The Convention also provides for the protection of critical habitat.

APPENDIX II. EXAMPLES OF MARINE REPTILE SYMBIONTS

Host	Symbiont	Type of Relationship	Gain From Host	Action Site
Generic Sea Turtle	Remora (*Echenesis* spp.)	Commensalism	Shelter, Transport	Plastron
	Barnacles (*Chelonibia* sp., *Chonchorderma* sp., *Lepas* sp., etc.)	Commensalism	Transport, Substrate	Carapace, Plastron
	Pilotfish (*Naucrates ductor*)	Mutualism	Transport, Protection, Food	Under Plastron
	Podocerid Amphipods (*Podocerus* spp.)	Parasitism	Food	Carapace
	Ozobranchus Leeches (*Ozobranchus* spp.)	Parasitism	Food (Blood)	Mouth
	Herbivorous Fish	Mutualism	Food (Algae)	Plastron, Carapace
	Seabirds	Commensalism	Resting Platform	Carapace
	Algae (Seaweeds)	Commensalism	Attachment Substrate	Carapace, Neck, Flippers, Head
Green Sea Turtle (*Chelonia mydas*)	Certain Reef Wrasses	Mutualism	Food (Barnacles)	Plastron, Neck, Groin
	Columbus Crabs (*Planes minutus*)	Mutualism	Food, Shelter	Tail, Cloaca, Hind Limbs
	Parasitic Barnacles (*Stephanolepas muricata*)	Parasitism	Food (Blood)	Plastron
	Commensal Barnacles (*Chelonibia testudinaria Platylepas hexastyles*)	Commensalism	Transport, Substrate	Skin, Neck, Head, Shell
Hawksbill Sea Turtle (*Eretmochelys imbricata*)	Columbus Crabs (*Planes minutus*)	Mutualism	Food, Shelter	Tail, Cloaca, Hind Limbs
Leatherback Sea Turtle (*Dermochelys coriacea*)	Trematodes (*Astrorchis renicapite*)	Parasitism	Food	Intestines
	Ameoba (*Entamoeba* sp.)	Parasitism	Food	Intestines
	Isopods (*Excollarana* sp.)	Parasitism	Food, Shelter	
Loggerhead Sea Turtle (*Caretta caretta*)	Columbus Crabs (*Planes minutus*)	Mutualism	Food, Shelter	Tail, Cloaca, Hind Limbs
	Mottled Shore Crabs (*Pachygrapsus* sp.)	Mutualism	Food, Shelter	Tail, Cloaca
	Common Mud Crabs (*Protopeus herbstii*)	Mutualism	Food, Shelter	Tail, Cloaca
	Say's Mud Crab (*Neopanope sayi*)	Mutualism	Food, Shelter	Tail, Cloaca
	Oyster (*Pinctada radiata*)	Commensalism	Transport, Substrate	
Olive Ridley Sea Turtle (*Lepidochelys olivacea*)	Barnacles (*Platylepas hexastylos, Chelonibia testudinaria*)	Commensalism	Transport, Substrate	Neck, Carapace Flippers
	Leech (*Ozobranchus* sp.)	Parasitism	Food	Neck, Flippers
	Crab (*Planes cyaneus*)	Mutualism	Food, Shelter	Carapace
Sea Snakes	Sea Snake Barnacle (*Platylepas ophiophilus*)	Commensalism	Transport, Substrate	Tail
Marine Iguana (*Amblyrhnchus cristatus*)	Ticks (*Ornithodoros* sp.)	Parasitism	Food	
	Assorted Fish	Mutualism	Food (Cleaning)	
Saltwater Crocodile	Filarial Worm	Parasitism	Food, Shelter	Intestine

APPENDIX III. GLOSSARY

Adult   At full size and strength; a sexually mature sea turtle.

Aphrodisiac   A food, drug or other agent, sometimes made from animal parts, that arouses sexual desire or enhances sexual performance.

Arribada   A unique nesting strategy, characterizing Kemp's and olive ridley sea turtles, where females approach the beach and nest *en masse*.

Basking   A behavior that exposes the body, or a portion of the body, to the warmth of the sun.

Benthic   Describing an organism that lives in the benthos, a biogeographical region referring to the bottom of an ocean, lake, or river.

Biomass   The amount of living matter in a given habitat, often expressed as the weight of organisms per unit area.

Body Pit   A depression dug by a female turtle where she settles while laying eggs.

Bycatch   Non-targeted organisms caught incidentally, or by accident, during fishing operations.

Calipee   Sea turtle cartilage; traditionally stewed with turtle meat to make soup.

Carapace   A bony shield or shell covering the dorsal (top) side of a turtle.

Carnivore   An animal that preys (feeds) on other animals; a meat-eater.

Caruncle   A temporary "egg tooth" (located on the hatchling's nose) used to break open the egg shell.

Chelonitoxin   A form of poison associated with consuming turtle meat from contaminated individuals.

Cloaca   The common cavity into which the intestinal, urinary and reproductive tracts open in reptiles and other animals; the opening through which sea turtle eggs are laid.

Clutch   The number of eggs produced by a turtle at one time.

Crop   A pouch in the esophagus of many birds (and Hawaiian green sea turtles), in which food is held for later digestion.

Dave   Great name for a kid or a co-author.

Diurnal   Occurring during the day, often in daily cycles.

Drift Lines   Elongated masses of seaweed, debris and other floating objects that often form where ocean currents converge (meet one another).

Ectothermic   An animal, including most reptiles, whose body temperature is determined largely by ambient (outside) temperature, as opposed to generating heat within its own body; what we used to call "cold-blooded".

Egg Chamber   A hole dug by an adult female turtle using her rear flippers, into which she lays her eggs.

Endangered Species   Under the U.S. Endangered Species Act, "Any species which is in danger of extinction throughout all or a significant portion of its range."

Endothermic   An animal (i.e bird or mammal) that can generate and maintain heat within its body independent of environmental temperature; what we used to call "warm blooded."

Epibiont   An organism living upon another organism, such as a barnacle attached to the shell of a sea turtle.

Feral   Animals (typically pets or livestock) that have reverted to a wild condition after escape or release from captivity.

Gizzard   An internal muscular structure that assists in grinding and breaking down food items.

Hatchling   Newly hatched turtle; yolk sac, or umbilical cord still visible.

Herbivore   An animal that feeds on plants.

Invertebrate   Any animal without a backbone.

Iteroparity   The strategy (successfully used by sea turtles) of reproducing many times during a lifetime.

Juvenile   Not at full size or strength; a sexually-immature sea turtle.

Myoglobin   An oxygen-binding protein in muscle tissue.

Niche   The ecological role of a species in its environment (defined by what it eats, who eats it, etc.)

Nocturnal   Occurring at night, such as with nesting by most species of sea turtle.

Omnivore   An animal that feeds on both plant and animal matter.

Oviparous   Offspring develop from fertilized eggs that hatch outside the mother.

Ovoviviparous   Offspring develop and hatch from fertilized eggs held within the oviduct of the mother.

Parasite   An organism that lives on or within a host from which it obtains nutrients and nourishment.

Pelagic   An organism living in the open ocean.

Pipping   The process by which a hatchling breaks free from the egg shell.

Plastron   The ventral (bottom) portion of a turtle's shell.

Predator   An animal that hunts and eats other animals.

Prehensile   Adapted for seizing, grasping or taking hold of things.

Salp   Free-swimming oceanic tunicate; a favorite food of the leatherback turtle.

Scale   Thin, flattened, plate-like structures that form the covering of certain animals, including turtles and other reptiles.

Scatophagy   The ingestion of feces in order to gain nutrition (through digestion of partially-broken down plant material) or inoculation of gut microfauna.

Scute   A horny plate, as on the shell of a turtle.

Spongivore   An organism, such as the hawksbill sea turtle, that specializes in feeding on sponges.

Territory   A defined area over which an organism maintains control and defends it against other organisms.

Threatened Species   Any species likely to become an endangered species within the foreseeable future throughout all or a significant portion of its range.

Trophic Levels   Each of the steps, or levels, in a food chain.

Turtle Excluder Device (TED)   A type of gear modification required for shrimp trawls operating in U. S. (and some other nations') waters, which releases turtles caught in trawl before they drown.

Vertebrate   Any animal with a backbone, including sea turtles and other reptiles.

APPENDIX IV. BIBLIOGRAPHY

This section is broken down into two parts, the first is broken down into subsections that list the primary references we used for each major section covered in 'Sea Turtles: An Ecological Guide'; and the second ("Want to Know More?") is a review of general books and booklets about sea turtles .

Adaptations

Standora, EA; Spotila, JR & Foley, RE (1982). Regional endothermy in the sea turtle, *Chelonia mydas*. *J. Therm. Biol.* 7(3): 159 – 165.

Anatomy

Work, TM (2000). Sea Turtle Necropsy Manual for Biologists in Remote Refuges. USGS, National Wildlife Health Center, Hawai'i Field Station, Honolulu. 25 pp.

Wyneken, J (2001). The Anatomy of Sea Turtles. NOAA Tech. Memo. NMFS-SEFSC-470. U.S. Dept. of Commerce, Miami. 172 pp.

Basking Behavior

Balazs, GH (1977). Ecological aspects of green turtles at Necker Island. Hawai'i Institute of Marine Biology. 27 pp.

Quiantance, JK; Rice MR & Balazs, GH (2002). Basking, foraging, and resting behavior of two sub-adult Green turtles in Kiholo Bay Lagoon, Hawai'i. *In*: Mosier, A; Foley, A & Frost, B (eds.). Proceedings of the Twentieth Annual Symposium on Sea Turtle Biology and Conservation. NOAA Tech. Memo NMFS-SEFSC-477.

Rice, MR; Balazs, GH; Kopra, D & Whittow, GC (2002). Ecology and behavior of Green turtles basking at Kiholo Bay, Hawai'i. *In*: Mosier, A; Foley, A & Frost, B (eds.). Proceedings of the Twentieth Annual Symposium on Sea Turtle Biology and Conservation. NOAA Tech. Memo NMFS-SEFSC-477. Pp. 153 – 155.

Sapsford, CW & van der Riet, M (1979). Uptake of solar radiation by the sea turtle *Caretta caretta*, during voluntary surface basking. *Comp. Biochem. Physiol.* 63A: 471 – 474.

Spotila, JR & Standora, EA (1985). Environmental constraints on the thermal energetics of sea turtles. *Copeia* 1985, 694.

Swimmer, JYB (1998). Physiological consequences of basking, disease and captivity in the green turtle, *Chelonia mydas*. *Diss. Abst. Int. Pt. B – Sci. & Eng.* 58(11): 5224.

Whittow, GC & Balazs, GH (1982). Basking behavior of the Hawaiian green turtle (*Chelonia mydas*). *Pac. Sci.* 36(2): 129 – 139.

Conservation

IUCN. 1980. World Conservation Strategy. Intl. Union for the Conservation of Nature and Natural Resources. Switz.

Frazier, JG (1999) Community-Based Conservation. *In*: Eckert, KL; Bjorndal, KA; Abreu-Grobois, FA; & Donnelly M (eds.). Research and Management Techniques for the Conservation of Sea Turtles, IUCN/SSC Marine Turtle Specialist Group Publication No. 4, 1999. Pp. 15 - 18.

Diet

Bjorndal, KA (1985). Nutritional ecology of sea turtles. *Copeia* 3: 736 - 751.

Eckert, SA (1992). Bound for deep water. *Natural History*, March 1992: 28 – 35.

Hartog, JC (1980). Notes on the food of sea turtles: *Eretmochelys imbricata* (Linnaeus) and *Dermochelys coriacea* (Linnaeus). *Neth. J. Zool.* 30(4): 595 – 610.

Meylan, A (1988). Spongivory in hawksbill turtles: a diet of glass. *Science* 239: 393 - 395.

Russell, DJ & Balazs GH (2000). Identification manual for dietary vegetation of the Hawaiian green turtle *Chelonia mydas*. US Dept. Commerce, NOAA Tech. Memo NMFS-SWFSC-294, Honolulu, HI. 49pp.

Diseases

Jacobson, ER; Behler, JL & Jarchow, JL (1998). Health assessment of chelonians and release into the wild. *In*: Fowler, ME & Miller, RE (eds.). Zoo and Wild Animal Medicine, Current Therapy 4. W. B. Saunders Co., Philadelphia, PA. Pp. 232 – 242.

Evolution

Dutton, PH; Davis SK; Guerra, T & Owens, D (1996). Molecular phylogeny for marine turtles based on sequences of the ND4-leucine tRNA and control regions of mitochondrial DNA. *Molecular Phylogenetics & Evol* 5(3): 511 – 521.

Hendrickson, JR (1980). The Ecological Strategies of Sea Turtles. *Amer. Zool.* 20: 597 – 608.

Wilbur, HM & Morin, PJ (1988). Life history evolution in turtles. *In*: Gans, C & Huey, RB (eds.). Biology of the Reptilia, Vol. 16 Ecology B: Defense and Life History. Alan R. Liss Inc., NY, NY. Pp. 387 - 440.

Feces

Balazs, GH; Fujioka, R & Fujioka C (1993). Marine turtle faeces on Hawaiian beaches. *Mar. Poll. Bull.* 26(7): 392 – 394.

Fibropapillomas & Other Diseases

Aquirre, AA; Spraker, TR; Balazs, GH & Zimmerman, B (1998). Spirorchidiasis and fibropapillomatosis in green turtles from the Hawaiian Islands. *J. Wildl. Dis.* 34: 91 – 98.

Balazs, GH & Pooley SG (eds). (1991). Research plan for marine turtle fibropapilloma. US Dept. Commerce, NOAA Tech. Memo NMFS-SWFSC-156, Honolulu, HI. 113pp.

Herbst, LH; Greiner, EC; Ehrhart, LM; Bagley, DA & Klein, PA (1998). Seriological association between spirorchidiasis, herpesvirus infection, and fibropapillomatosis in green turtles from Florida. *J. Wildl. Dis.* 34(3): 496 – 507.

Herbst, LH & Jacobson ER(1995). Diseases of marine turtles. *In*: Bjorndal, KA (ed.). Biology and Conservation of Sea Turtles. Smithsonian Institution Press, Washington D.C. Pp 593 – 596.

Klein, PA (1998). Association of a unique chelonid herpesvirus with sea turtle fibropapillomas. *Mar. Turtle Newsl.* 80: 14.

Lu, Y; Nerurkar, VR; Aguirre, AA; Work, TM; Balazs, GH & Yanagihara, R (1999). Establishment and characterization of 13 cell lines from a green sea turtle (*Chelonia mydas*) with fibropapillomas. *In Vitro Cell. Dev. Biol Anim.* 35(7): 389 – 393.

Quackenbush, SL; Work, TM; Balazs, GH; Casey, RN; Rovnak, J; Chaves, A; duToit, L; Baines, JD; Parrish, CR; Bowser, PR & Casey, JW (1998). Three closely related herpesviruses are associated with fibropapillomatosis in marine turtles. *Virology* 246(2): 392 – 399.

Fishing

Eckert, SA & Sarti, LM (1997). Distant fisheries implicated in the loss of the world's largest leatherback nesting population. *Mar. Turtle Newsl.* 78: 2 – 7.

Frazier, J & Montero, JLB (1990). Incidental capture of marine turtles by the swordfish fishery at San Antonio, Chile. *Mar. Turtle Newsl.* 49: 8 – 13.

Gerosa, G & Casale, P (1999). Interaction of Marine Turtles with Fisheries in the Mediterranean. UNEP Regional Activity Centre for Specially Protected Areas, Tunisia. 59 pp.

Flatback Sea Turtles

Limpus, CJ; Couper, PJ & Couper, KLD (1993). Crab Island: Reassessment of the world's largest flatback turtle rookery after twelve years. *Memoirs of the Qld Museum* 33(1): 277 - 289.

Limpus, CJ; Zeller, D; Kwan, D and MacFarlane, W (1989). Sea-turtle rookeries in North-western Torres Strait. *Aust. Wildl. Res.* 16: 517 - 525.

Walker, TA & Parmenter, CJ (1990). Absence of a pelagic phase in the life cycle of the flatback turtle, *Natator depressus* (Garman). *J. Biogeogr.* 17: 275 – 278.

Zangerl, R, Hendrickson, LP and Hendrickson, JR (1988). A Redescription of the Australian Flatback Sea Turtle, Natator depressus. Bishop Museum Bulletin in Zoology I. Bishop Museum Press, Honolulu, HI. 69 pp.

Geographical Distributions

Márquez, MR (1990). FAO Species Catalogue. Vol. 11: Sea Turtles of the World. An Annotated and Illustrated Catalogue of Sea Turtle Species Known to Date. FAO Fisheries Synopsis. No. 125. Rome, FAO. 81 pp.

Green Sea Turtles

Balazs, GH (1977). Ecological aspects of green turtles at Necker Island. Hawai'i Institute of Marine Biology. 27 pp.

Balazs, GH (1995). Growth rates of immature green turtles in the Hawaiian archipelago. *In*: Bjorndal, KA (ed.). Biology and Conservation of Sea Turtles, Revised Edition. Smithsonian Institution Press, Washington D.C. Pp 117 – 125.

Hirth, HF (1997). Synopsis of the Biological Data on the Green Turtle *Chelonia mydas* (Linnaeus 1758). Biological Report 97(1). U.S. Fish & Wildlife Service, Washington D.C. 120 pp.

National Marine Fisheries Service and U. S. Fish & Wildlife Service (1998). Recovery Plan for U. S. Pacific populations of the East Pacific Green Turtle (*Chelonia mydas*). National Marine Fisheries Service, Silver Spring, MD. 50 pp.

National Marine Fisheries Service and U. S. Fish & Wildlife Service (1998). Recovery Plan for U. S. Pacific populations of the Green Turtle (*Chelonia mydas*). National Marine Fisheries Service, Silver Spring, MD. 84 pp.

Seminoff, JA; Resendiz, A; Nichols, WJ & Jones, TT (2002). Growth rates of wild green turtles (*Chelonia mydas*) at a temperate foraging habitat in the Gulf of California, Mexico. *Copiea* 2002: 610 - 617.

Zug, GR; Balazs, GH; Wetherall, JA; Parker, DM & Murakawa, SKK (2002). Age and growth of Hawaiian green sea turtles (*Chelonia mydas*): an analysis based on skeletochronology. *Fisheries Bulletin* 100: 117 - 127.

Habitat

Bouchard, SS & Bjorndal, KA (2000). Sea turtles as biological transporters of nutrients and energy from marine to terrestrial ecosystems. *Ecology* 81(8): 2305 – 2313.

Hatchlings

Bustard, HR (1970). The significance of coloration in hatchling green sea turtles. *Herpetologica* 26(2): 224 – 227.

Carr, AF & Hirth, H (1961). Social facilitation in green sea turtle siblings. *Anim. Behav.* 9: 68.

Fretey, J (1981). Tortues marines de Guyane. Ed. Du Léopard d'Or, Paris. 136 pp.

Goff, M; Salmon, M & Lohmann, KJ (1998). Hatchling sea turtles use surface waves to establish a magnetic compass direction. *Anim. Behav.* 55(1): 69 – 71.

Lohmann, KJ (1992). How sea turtles navigate. *Scientific American*, January: 100 - 106.

Lohmann, KJ & Fittinghoff-Lohmann, CM (1993). A light-independent magnetic compass in the leatherback sea turtle. *Biol. Bull.* 185(1): 149 – 151.

Lohmann, KJ; Witherington, BE; Lohmann, CMF & Salmon, M (1997). Orientation, navigation, and natal beach homing in sea turtles. *In*: Lutz, PL & Musick, JA (eds.). The Biology of Sea Turtles. CRC Press, Boca Raton, FL. Pp. 107 - 163.

Miller, JD (1997). Reproduction in Sea Turtles. *In*: Lutz, PL & Musick, JA (eds.). The Biology of Sea Turtles. CRC Press, Boca Raton, FL. Pp. 68 - 69.

Salmon, M & Wyeneken, J (1994). Orientation by hatchling sea turtles: mechanisms and implications. *Herpetological Natural History* 2(1): 13 - 24.

Salmon, M; Wyneken, J; Fritz, E & Lucas, M (1992). Seafinding by hatchling sea turtles: Role of brightness, silhouette and beach slope as orientation cues. *Behav.* 122: 56 – 77.

Wang, JH; Jackson, JK & Lohmann, KJ (1998). Perception of wave surge motion by hatchling sea turtles. *J. Exp. Mar. Biol. Ecol.* 229(2): 177 - 186.

Wyneken, J & Salmon, M (1992). Frenzy and post-frenzy swimming activity in loggerhead, green, and leatherback hatchling sea turtles. *Copiea* 1(2): 478 – 484.

Hawksbill Sea Turtles

Limpus, CJ (1987). Sea Turtles. *In*: Covacevich, J; Davie, P & Pearn, J (eds.). Toxic Plants and Animals: A Guide for Australia. Red Velvet, Brisbane, Australia. Pp. 189 - 193.

Meylan, A (1988). Spongivory in hwksbill turtles: a diet of glass. *Science* 139: 393 - 395.

Thomas, C & Scott, S (1997). All Stings Considered: First Aid and Medical Treatment of Marine Injuries. University of Hawai'i Press, Honolulu, HI. Pp. 150 - 153.

Witzell, WN (1983). Synopsis of Biological Data on the Hawksbill Sea Turtle, *Eretmochelys imbricata* (Linnaeus, 1766), FAO Fisheries Synopsis No. 137. Rome, Italy. 78 pp.

National Marine Fisheries Service and U. S. Fish & Wildlife Service (1998). Recovery Plan for U. S. Pacific populations of the Hawksbill Turtle (*Eretmochelys imbricata*). National Marine Fisheries Service, Silver Spring, MD. 82 pp.

Human Impacts

Balazs, GH & Pooley, SG (1993) Report plan to assess marine turtle hooking mortality: results of an expert workshop held in Honolulu. U. S. Dept. of Commerce AJM Report H : 93-18.

Bjorndal, KA; Bolten, AB & Lagueux, CJ (1994). Ingestion of marine debris by juvenile sea turtles in coastal Florida habitats. *Mar. Pollut. Bull.* 28(3): 154 - 158.

Fritts, TH & McGehee, MA (1989). Effects of petroleum on the development and survival of marine turtle embryos. Proc. 2nd Western Atl. Turtle Symp., Oct. 12 – 16, 1987, Mayaguez, Puerto Rico. Pp. 321 – 322.

Gerrior, P (1996). Incidental take of sea turtles in the northeast longline fishery – sea turtle interactions. Proc. Pelagic Longline Fishery – Sea Turtle Interactions Workshop. NOAA Tech. Memo. NMFS-OPR. 73 pp.

Gordon, AN; Pople, AR & Ng, J (1998). Trace metal concentrations in livers and kidneys of sea turtles from south-eastern Queensland, Australia. *Mar. Freshwat. Res.* 49(5): 409 – 414.

Lutcavage, ME; Lutz, PL; Bossart, GD & Hudson, DM (1995). Physiologic and clinicopathologic effects of crude oil on loggerhead sea turtles. *Arch. Environ. Contam. Toxicol.* 28: 417 - 422.

Lutz, PL and Lutcavage, M (1989). The effects of petroleum on sea turtles: applicability to Kemp's Ridley. *In*: Caillouet, CW and Landry, AM (eds.). First Int'l Symp. on Kemp's Ridley Sea Turtle Biology, Conservation and Mgmt. TAMU - SG89-105: 52-54. Galveston.

Pegendarm, W (1992). Turtles slow dredging projects. *South. Ship.* 41(3): 12 – 13.

Witherington, BE & Martin, RE (2000). Understanding, Assessing, and Resolving Light-Pollution Problems on Sea Turtle Nesting Beaches (Revised edition). Florida Fish and Wildlife Conservation Commission, FMRI Technical Report TR-2, Tallahassee. 73 pp.

Witzell, WN (1994). The origin, evolution, and demise of the U. S. sea turtle fisheries. *Mar. Fish. Rev.* 56(4): 8 – 23.

Juvenile Sea Turtles

Eckert, SA (2002). Distribution of juvenile leatherback sea turtle *Dermochelys coriacea* sightings. *Mar Ecol Progr Ser* 230: 289 - 293.

Musick, JA & Limpus, CJ (1997). Habitat Utilization in Juvenile Sea Turtles. *In*: Lutz, PL & Musick, JA (eds.). The Biology of Sea Turtles. CRC Press, Boca Raton, FL. Pp. 137 - 155.

Kemp's Ridley Sea Turtles

Marquez, MR (1994). Synopsis of Biological Data on the Kemp's Ridley Turtle, *Lepidochelys kempi* (Garman, 1880). NOAA Tech. Memo. NMFS-SEFSC-343. 91 pp.

Rostal, DC; Grumbles, JC; Byles, RA; Marquez MR & Owens, DW (1997). Nesting physiology of Kemp's ridley sea turtles, *Lepidochelys kempi*, at Rancho Nuevo, Tamaulipas, Mexico, with observations on population estimates. *Chelonian Conservation and Biology* 2(4): 538 - 547.

Weber, M (1995). Kemp's Ridley Sea Turtle, *Lepidochelys kempii*. *In*: Plotkin, PT (ed). Status Reviews for Sea Turtles Listed under the Endangered Species Act of 1973. NOAA/National Marine Fisheries Service, Silver Spring and U.S. Fish and Wildlife Service, Bethesda. Pp 109 – 122.

Keystone Species

Aragones, LV (2000). A review of the role of the green turtle in tropical seagrass ecosystems. *In*: Pilcher N & Ismail G (eds.). Sea Turtles of the Indo-Pacific: Research, Management & Conservation. Pp. 69 – 85.

Leatherback Sea Turtles

Eckert, SA (1992). Bound for deep water. *Natural History*, March 1992: 28 – 35.

Eckert, SA, Eckert, KL, Ponganis, P & Kooyman, GL (1989). Diving and foraging behavior by leatherback sea turtles (*Dermochelys coriacea*). *Canadian Journal of Zoology* 67:2834-2840.

Eckert, SA (2002). Swim speed and movement patterns of gravid leatherbacks at St. Croix, U.S. Virgin Islands. *J. Exp. Biol.* 205: 3689-3697.

Heng, CE & Chark, LH (1989). The Leatherback Turtle: A Malaysian Heritage. Tropical Press Sdn. Bhd. Kuala Lumpur, Malaysia. 49 pp.

National Marine Fisheries Service and U. S. Fish & Wildlife Service (1998). Recovery Plan for U. S. Pacific Populations of the Leatherback Turtle (*Dermochelys coriacea*). National Marine Fisheries Service, Silver Spring, MD. 65 pp.

Locomotion

Walker, WF Jr (1979). Locomotion, *In*: Harless, M & Morlock M (eds). Turtles: Perspectives and Research. John Wiley & Sons, Inc. NY. Pp. 435 – 454.

Wyneken, J (1997). Sea turtle locomotion: mechanisms, behavior, and energetics. *In*: Lutz, PL & Musick, JA (eds.). The Biology of Sea Turtles. CRC Press, Boca Raton, FL. Pp. 165 – 198.

Loggerhead Sea Turtles

Jurado, LFL; Pérez, MC & Martel, VM (2000). The Common Turtle in the Canary Islands. Gobierno de Canarias, Consejería de Política Territorial Vice Consejería de Medio Ambiente. GC-1518/2000. 15 pp.

National Marine Fisheries Service (1990). Draft Recovery Plan for U. S. Pacific Populations of the Loggerhead Turtle (*Caretta caretta*). National Marine Fisheries Service, St. Petersburg, FL.

National Marine Fisheries Service and U. S. Fish & Wildlife Service (1998). Recovery Plan for U. S. Pacific populations of the Loggerhead Turtle (*Caretta caretta*). National Marine Fisheries Service, Silver Spring, MD. 59 pp

Management

Caillouet, CW; Revera, DB; Duronslet, MJ & Brucks, J (1989). Dermatoglyphic patterns on Kemp's ridley sea turtle flippers: Can they be used to identify individuals? *Proc. 1st Int'l Symp. Kemp's Ridley Sea Turtle Biol., Cons. & Mgmt, Oct. 1 – 4, 1985, Galveston, Texas.* Pp. 146 – 150.

Kinan, I (ed.). (2002). Proceedings of the Western Pacific Sea Turtle Cooperative Research and Management Workshop. February 5 – 8, 2002, Honolulu, HI. Western Pacific Regional Fisheries Management Council. 300 pp.

National Marine Fisheries Service (1980). 'Living tags' for sea turtles. U. S. Dept. of Commerce, Southwest Fish. Cent. NOAA Tech. Memo. 29 pp.

National Marine Fisheries Service (1999). Our living oceans. Report on the status of U. S. living marine resources, 1999. U. S. Dept. of Commerce, NOAA Tech. Memo. NMFS-F/SPO-41. 301 pp.

Marine Iguanas

Trillmich, KGK (1983). The mating system of the marine iguana (*Amblyrhynchus cristatus*). *J. Comp. Ethology* 63: 141 – 172.

Wikelski, M (1999). Influences of parasites and thermoregulation on grouping tendencies in marine iguanas. *Behav. Ecol.* 10: 22 – 29

Wikelski, M; Carrillo, V & Trillmich, F (1997). Energy limits to body size in a grazing reptile, the Galapagos marine iguana. *Ecology* 78(7): 2204 – 2217.

Marine Reptiles

McKeown, S (1996). A Field guide to Reptiles and Amphibians in the Hawaiian Islands. Diamond Head Publishing, Inc. Los Osos, CA. 172 pp.

Zug, GR (1993). Herpetology: An Introduction to the Biology of Amphibians and Reptiles. Academic Press, Inc. San Diego, CA. 527 pp.

Mating

Fitzsimmons, NN (1998). Single paternity of clutches and sperm storage in the promiscuous green turtle (*Chelonia mydas*). *Mol. Ecol.* 7(5): 575 – 584.

Kichler, K; Holder, MT; Davis, SK; Marquez-M., R & Owens, DW (1999). Detection of multiple paternity in the Kemp's ridley sea turtle with limited sampling. *Mol. Ecol.* 8: 819 – 830.

Monitoring

Balazs, GH (1999). Factors to consider in the tagging of sea turtles. *In:* Eckert, KL; Bjorndal, KA; Abreu-Grobois, FA; & Donnelly M (eds.). Research and Management Techniques for the Conservation of Sea Turtles, IUCN/SSC Marine Turtle Specialist Group Publication No. 4, Pp. 101 – 109.

Eckert, SA (1999). Data acquisition systems for monitoring sea turtle behavior and physiology. *In:* Eckert, KL; Bjorndal, KA; Abreu-Grobois, FA; & Donnelly M (eds.). Research and Management Techniques for the Conservation of Sea Turtles, IUCN/SSC Marine Turtle Specialist Group Publication No. 4, Pp. 88 – 93.

Natural Sources of Stress

Cornelius, SE (1986). The Sea Turtles of Santa Rosa National Park. Fundación de Parques Nacionales. San José, Costa Rica. 64 pp.

Ratnaswamy, MJ, Warren, RJ, Kramer, MT, & Adam, MD (1997). Comparisons of lethal and nonlethal techniques to reduce raccoon depredation of sea turtle nests. *J. Wild. Management* 61(2): 368 - 376.

Nesting

Ackerman, RA (1980). Physiological and ecological aspects of gas exchange by sea turtle eggs. *Am. Zool.* 20(3): 575 – 583.

Hirth, HF (1980). Some aspects of the nesting behavior and reproductive biology of sea turtles. *Am. Zool.* 20(3): 507 – 523.

Kuchling, G (1998). The Reproductive Biology of the *Chelonia*. Springer-Verlag, Berlin. 223 pp.

Miller, JD (1997). Reproduction in Sea Turtles. *In:* Lutz, PL & Musick, JA (eds.). The Biology of Sea Turtles. CRC Press, Boca Raton, FL. Pp. 51 - 81

Mortimer, JA (1982). Factors influencing beach selection by nesting sea turtles. *In:* Bjorndal, KA (ed.). Biology and Conservation of Sea Turtles. Smithsonian Institution Press, Washington D. C. Pp. 45 - 51.

Poland, RHC (1996). EuroTurtle: Species Distribution Sections Web Pages. www.org/EuroTurtle.

Schroeder, B & Murphy, S (1999). Population surveys (ground and aerial) on Nesting Beaches. *In:* Eckert, KL; Bjorndal, KA; Abreu-Grobois, FA; & Donnelly M (eds.). Research and Management Techniques for the Conservation of Sea Turtles, IUCN/SSC Marine Turtle Specialist Group Publication No. 4, Pp. 45 – 55.

Olive Ridley Sea Turtles

National Marine Fisheries Service and U. S. Fish & Wildlife Service (1998). Recovery Plan for U. S. Pacific populations of the Olive Ridley Turtle (*Lepidochelys olivacea*). National Marine Fisheries Service, Silver Spring, MD. 52 pp.

Predators

Audesirk, T & Audesirk, G (1996). Biology: Life on Earth, 4th ed. Prentice-Hall, Upper Saddle River, NJ. Pp. 336.

Gyuris, E (1994). The rate of predation by fishes on hatchlings of the green turtle (*Chelonia mydas*). *Coral Reefs* 13(3): 137 – 144.

Sea Snakes

Dunson, WA (ed.). (1975). The Biology of Sea Snakes. University Park Press, Baltimore. 530 pp.

Heatwole, H (1978). Adaptations of marine snakes. *Am. Sci.* 66(5): 594 – 604.

Preide, M (1990). The sea snakes are coming. *New Scientist* 128:29 – 33.

Vallarino, O & Weldon, PJ (1996). Reproduction in the yellow-bellied sea snake (*Pelamis platurus*) from Panama: Field and laboratory observations. *Zoo Biol.* 15(3): 309 – 314.

Voris, HK & Voris, HH (1983). Feeding strategies in marine snakes: an analysis of evolutionary, morphological, behavioral and ecological relationships. *Amer. Zool.* 23(2): 411 - 425.

Zimmerman, K & Heatwole, H (1990). Cutaneous photoreception: a new sensory mechanism for reptiles. *Copeia* 3: 860 - 862.

Sex Determination

Ackerman, RA (1997). The nest environment and the embryonic development of sea turtles. *In:* Lutz, PL & Musick, JA (eds.). The Biology of Sea Turtles. CRC Press, Boca Raton, FL. Pp. 83 – 106.

Symbionts

Balazs, GH (1981). Sea turtles as natural fish aggregating devices. *Hawai'i Fishing News* 6:5.

Davenport, J (1994). A cleaning association between the oceanic crab *Planes minutus* and the loggerhead sea turtle *Caretta caretta*. *J. Mar. Biol. Assoc. UK* 74(3): 735 – 737.

Frazier, JG, Fiestine, HL, Beavers, SC, Achavel, F, Suganuma, H, Pitman, RL, Yamaguchi, Y & Prigioni, CM (1994). Impalement of marine turtles (Reptilia, Chelonia: Cheloniidae and Dermochelyidae) by billfishes (Osteichthyes, Perciformes: Istophoridae and Xiphiidae). *Envir. Biol. Fishes* 39: 85 – 96.

Frick, MG, Williams, KL & Veljacic, D (2000). Additional evidence supporting a cleaning association between epibiotic crabs and sea turtles: how will the harvest of sargassum seaweed impact this relationship? *Mar. Turtle Newsl.* 90: 11 – 13.

Lauckner, G (1985). Diseases of Reptilia. Diseases of Marine Animals. Vol. 4, Pt. 2. Introduction, Reptilia, Aves, Mammalia. Pp. 553 – 626.

Pitman, RL (1993). Seabird associations with marine turtles in the eastern Pacific Ocean. *Colonial Waterbirds* 16(2): 194 – 201.

Zamzow, JP (1999). Cleaning symbiosis between Hawaiian reef fishes and green sea turtles, *Chelonia mydas*, with and without fibropapillomas. Masters Thesis. Department of Zoology, University of Hawai'i, Honolulu, HI. 43 pp.

Zann, LP (1980). Living Together in the Sea. T. F. H. Publications, Neptune, NJ. 416 pp.

Traditional Uses/Turtle Products

Chacón, DC (2002). Diagnóstico sobre el comercio de las tortugas marinas y sus derivados en el Istmo Centroamericano. Red Regional para la Conservación de las Tortugas Marinas en Centroamérica (RCA). San José, Costa Rica. 247 pp.

Johannes, RE (1986). A review of information on the subsistence use of green and hawksbill sea turtles on islands under United States jurisdiction in the western Pacific Ocean. National Marine Fisheries Service Administrative Report SWR-86-2. 41 pp.

McNamee, G & Urrea, LA (eds) (1996). A World of Turtles: A Literary Celebration. Johnson Books, Boulder, Colorado. 149 pp.

Turtle Excluder Devices (TEDs)

Crowder, LB; Hopkins-Murphy, SR & Royle, JA (1995). *In*: Bjorndal, KA (ed.). Biology and Conservation of Sea Turtles. Smithsonian Institution Press, Washington D.C. 615 pp.

Henwood, TA & Stuntz, WE (1987). Analysis of sea turtle captures and mortalities during commercial shrimp trawling. *Fish. Bull.* 85: 813 – 817.

Turtle Tracks

Miller, JD (1997). Reproduction In Sea Turtles. *In:* Lutz, PL & Musick, JA (eds.). The Biology of Sea Turtles. CRC Press, Boca Raton, FL. Pp. 59 - 60.

Schroeder, B & Murphy, S (1999). Population Surveys (Ground and Aerial) on Nesting Beaches. *In:* Eckert, KL; Bjorndal, KA; Abreu-Grobois, FA & Donnelly, M (eds.). Research and Management Techniques for the Conservation of Sea Turtles. IUCN/SSC Marine Turtle Specialist Publication No. 4. Pp. 45 – 55.

WANT TO KNOW MORE?

There are dozens of excellent books available on sea turtles. We have selected a handful of references to get you started, representing sea turtle literature from around the world. We hope you will enjoy learning more about these ancient and mysterious creatures!

Bjorndal, KA (ed.). (1995). Biology and Conservation of Sea Turtles, Revised Edition. Smithsonian Institution Press, Washington D.C. 615 pp.

Bolton, AB & Witherington, BE (eds.) (2003). Loggerhead Sea Turtles. Smithsonian Books, Washington, DC. 319 pp.

Carr, A (1967). The Sea Turtle: So Excellent a Fishe. University of Texas Press, Austin. 280 pp.

Dash, MC & Kar, CS (1990). The Turtle Paradise: Gahirmatha. Interprint, New Delhi. 295 pp.

Davidson, OG (2001). Fire in the Turtle House: The Green Sea Turtle and the Fate of the Ocean. Public Affairs, New York. 258 pp.

Eckert, KL (1993). The Biology and Population Status of Marine Turtles in the North Pacific Ocean. NOAA Technical Memorandum NMFS-SWFSC-186. U.S. Dept. Commerce. National Marine Fisheries Service, Honolulu. 156 pp.

Eckert, KL; Bjorndal, KA; Abreu-Grobois FA & Donnelly, M (eds.). (1999). Research and Management Techniques for the Conservation of Sea Turtles. IUCN/SSC Marine Turtle Specialist Group Publ. No. 4. Washington, D.C. 235 pp.

Fleming, EH (2001). Swimming Against the Tide: Recent Surveys of Exploitation, Trade and Management of Marine Turtles in the Northern Caribbean. TRAFFIC North America. Washington D.C. 161 pp.

Frazier, J (1985). Marine Turtles in the Comoro Archipelago. North-Holland Publ. Company, Amsterdam. 177 pp.

Fretey, J (2001). Biogeography and Conservation of Marine Turtles of the Atlantic Coast of Africa. Convention on Migratory Species Technical Series Publ. No. 6. Bonn, Germany. 429 pp.

Groombridge, B & Luxmoore, R (1989). The Green Turtle and Hawksbill (Reptilia: Cheloniidae): World Status, Exploitation and Trade. CITES Secretariat, Lausanne, Switzerland. 601 pp.

Klemens, MW (ed). (2000). Turtle Conservation. Smithsonian Institution Press. 334 pp.

Lindsay, C & Watcon, L (1995). Turtles Islands: Balinese Ritual and the Green Turtle. Takarajima Books, New York. 119 pp.

Lutz, PL; Musick, JA & Wyneken, J (eds.). (2003). The Biology of Sea Turtles, Volume II. CRC Press, Boca Raton, Florida. 455 pp.

Lutz, PL & Musick, JA (eds.). (1997). The Biology of Sea Turtles. CRC Press, Boca Raton, Florida. 432 pp.

National Research Council (1990). Decline of the Sea Turtles. National Academy Press, Washington D.C. 259 pp.

O'Keefe, MT (1995). Sea Turtles: The Watchers' Guide. Larsen's Outdoor Publishing, Lakeland, Florida. 128 pp.

Phillips, P (1989). The Great Ridley Rescue. Mountain Press Publishing Company, Missoula, Montana. 180 pp.

Pilcher, N & Ismail, G (eds). (2000). Sea Turtles of the Indo-Pacific: Research, Management and Conservation. ASEAN Academic Press, London. 361 pp.

Plotkin, PT (ed.). (1995). Status Reviews for Sea Turtles under the Endangered Species Act of 1973. National Marine Fisheries Service, Silver Spring, MD. 140 pp.

Pritchard, PCH and Trebbau, P (1984). The Turtles of Venezuela. Society for the Study of Amphibians and Reptiles. 468 pp.

Rebel, TP (1974). Sea Turtles and the Turtle Industry of the West Indies, Florida and the Gulf of Mexico. Revised Edition. Univ. Miami Press. 250 pp.

Ripple, J (1996). Sea Turtles. Voyageur Press, Stillwater, MN. 84 pp.

Rudloe, J (1995). Search for the Great Turtle Mother. Pineapple Press, Inc. Sarasota, FL. 271 pp.

Van Meter, VB (2002). Florida's Sea Turtles, 2nd ed. Florida Power and Light Company, Tallahassee. 60 pp.

Weber, M; Crouse, D, Irvin R & Iudicello, S (1995). Delay and Denial: A Political History of Sea Turtles and Shrimp Fishing. Center for Marine Conservation [*now The Ocean Conservancy*], Washington D.C. 45 pp.

Wyneken, J (2001). The Anatomy of Sea Turtles. NOAA Tech. Mem. NMFS-SEFSC-470. U. S. Dept. Commerce, Miami. 172 pp.

WEB PAGES

Anatomy of Sea Turtles
    http://courses.science.fau.edu/~jwyneken/sta/

Caribbean Conservation Corporation and Sea Turtle Survival League
    www.cccturtle.org/ccctmp.htm

CMS Marine Turtle Activities
    www.wcmc.org.uk/cms/turtles_intermedpage_index.htm

Euroturtle
    www.euroturtle.org

Marinelife Center of Juno Beach
    www.floridaleatherbacks.com.
    www.marinelife.org

Marine Turtle Fibropapilloma Bibliography
    www.turtles.org/nmfsbib.htm

Marine Turtle Newsletter
    www.seaturtle.org/mtn

Orientation Mechanisms in Young Sea Turtles
    www.unc.edu/depts/geomag

Proceedings of the Annual Symposia on Sea Turtle Biology and Conservation
    www.nmfs.noaa.gov/prot_res/PR3/Turtles/symposia.html

Recovery Plans
    USA:
    www.nmfs.noaa.gov/prot_res/PR3/recovery.html
    Australia:
    www.deh.gov.au/coasts/species/turtles/recovery/index.html
    Wider Caribbean:
    www.cep.unep.org/pubs/techreports/techreports.html

SeaTurtle.org
    www.seaturtle.org

Sea Turtles in Indian Ocean and Southeast Asia
    http://www.ioseaturtles.org/

TurtleTrax
    www.turtles.org

Wider Caribbean Sea Turtle Conservation Network (WIDECAST)
    www.widecast.org

APPENDIX V. GENERAL INDEX

About the Authors:

Dave Gulko

Dave Gulko is a coral reef ecologist who manages coral reefs for the State of Hawai'i Department of Land and Natural Resources. He actively works in the fields of tropical marine ecosystems, marine alien species, marine protected areas and marine endangered species.

He is the author of the popular book 'Hawaiian Coral Reef Ecology' and numerous scientific and popular articles about tropical marine ecosystems and natural resource management. He has served on national working groups for the U.S. Coral Reef Task Force and the U.S. Aquatic Nuisance Species Task Force. An expert on Hawaiian coral reefs, he has actively developed marine education [ ] ondary, university and non[ ] for over two decades.

His view of the world, as ex[ ] is that we need to endeavor[ ] nections between animals[ ] ment, and strive to control[ ] ences on the vital ecolog[ ] sustain us all.

Karen Eckert

Dr. Karen L. Eckert has been active for more than two decades in the fields of sea turtle research and international conservation policy. She is currently Executive Director of the Wider Caribbean Sea Turtle Conservation Network (WIDECAST). For her work as Executive Director of WIDECAST, Dr. Eckert was inducted into the "Global 500 Roll of Honour for Environmental Achievement" by the United Nations in 1994. UNEP has characterized her as "one of the most important figures in conservation and grassroots community empowerment in the field of endangered species in the Wider Caribbean Region."

[ ] her work with WIDECAST, Dr. [ ]lished numerous scientific and [ ] articles, technical manuals, and [ ]ts related to sea turtles and their [ ] She is a member of the U.S. [ ] Atlantic/Caribbean Sea Turtle [ ]s, and the Marine Turtle Spe- [ ] of the IUCN Species Survival

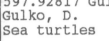
© David Schrichte

If you enjoyed 'Sea Turtles: An Ecological Guide', you might want to check out 'Hawaiian Coral Reef Ecology' also published by Mutual Publishing.

If you are a teacher who is adopting this book for classroom purposes, you may be eligible for a free copy of 'Sea Turtles: An Ecological Guide Teacher's Activity Booklet'; contact Mutual Publishing for more information.

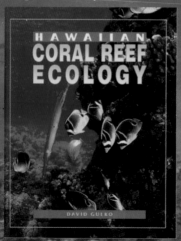

HAWAIIAN
CORAL REEF ECOLOGY

DAVID GULKO

SEA TURTLES
AN ECOLOGICAL GUIDE

TEACHER'S ACTIVITY BOOKLET

Dave Gulko
and
Karen Eckert